The Wagner Story Book

FIRELIGHT TALES OF
THE GREAT MUSIC DRAMAS

Henry Frost

The Wagner Story Book
Henry Frost

© 1st World Library – Literary Society, 2004
PO Box 2211
Fairfield, IA 52556
www.1stworldlibrary.org
First Edition

LCCN: 2003195023

ISBN: 1-59540-306-X

Purchase *"The Wagner Story Book"*
as a traditional bound book at:
www.1stWorldLibrary.org/purchase.asp?ISBN=1-59540-306-X

1st World Library Literary Society is a nonprofit organization dedicated to promoting literacy by:

- Creating a free internet library accessible from any computer worldwide.
- Hosting writing competitions and offering book publishing scholarships.

Readers interested in supporting literacy through sponsorship, donations or membership please contact:
literacy@1stworldlibrary.org
Check us out at: www.1stworldlibrary.org

The Wagner Story Book
*contributed by the Charles Family
in support of
1st World Library Literary Society*

CONTENTS

THE STOLEN TREASURE…………………….7

THE DAUGHTER OF THE GOD……………..26

THE HERO WHO KNEW NO FEAR……………41

THE END OF THE RING…………………..58

THE KNIGHT OF THE SWAN…………………73

THE PRIZE OF A SONG…………………...86

THE BLOOD-RED SAIL…………………….105

THE LOVE POTION……………………….120

THE MINSTREL KNIGHT………………….138

THE KING OF THE GRAIL………………….153

THE ASHES…………………………….172

THE STOLEN TREASURE

There is a certain little girl who sometimes tries to find out when I am not over busy, so that she may ask me to tell her a story. She is kind enough to say that she likes my stories, and this so flatters my vanity that I like nothing better than telling them to her. One reason why she likes them, I suspect, is that they are not really my stories at all, the most of them. They are the stories that the whole world has known and loved all these hundreds and thousands of years, tales of the gods and the heroes, of the giants and the goblins. Those are the right stories to tell to children, I believe, and the right ones for children to hear - the wonderful things that used to be done, up in the sky, and down under the ocean, and inside the mountains. If the boys and girls do not find out now, while they are young, all about the strange, mysterious, magical life of the days when the whole world was young, it is ten to one that they will never find out about it at all, for the most of us do not keep ourselves like children always, though surely we have all been told plainly enough that that is what we ought to do.

This little girl's mother is rather a strange sort of woman. I do not know that she exactly disagrees with us about these stories that we both like so much, but she seems to have a different way of looking at them from ours. I sometimes suspect that she does not even believe in fairies at all, that she never so much as thought she saw a ghost, that, if she heard a dozen wild horses galloping over the roof of the house and then flying away into the sky, she would think it was only the wind, and that she is no more afraid of ogres than of policemen. Still she is a woman whom one cannot help liking, in some respects.

But one day she said something to the little girl that surprised me, and made me think that perhaps I had done her injustice. The child came to me with a face full of perplexity and said: "What do you suppose mamma just told me?"

"I am sure I can't guess," I replied; "your mother tells you such ridiculous things that I am always afraid to think what will be the next. Perhaps she says that William Tell didn't shoot an apple off his little boy's head, or that the baker's wife didn't box King Alfred's ears for letting the cakes burn."

"Oh, no," said the child, "it isn't a bit like that; she says that you can see pictures in the fire sometimes - men and horses and trees and all kinds of things."

"Does she, indeed? And how does your mother know what I can see in the fire or what I can't see?"

"Oh, I don't mean just you - yourself, I mean anybody. Now can you? I mean can anybody?"

"Why, yes, if that is what you mean; I think some people can. It is the most sensible thing I have known your mother to say in a long time."

"But how can anybody see such things? Can you see

them? I have been looking at the fire ever so long, and I can't see anything at all but just the fire, the wood, and the ashes."

"Let us look at it together," I said; and I put a chair that was big enough to hold both of us before the fireplace. "Just see how bright the fire is; look down into those deep places under the sticks, and see how it glows and shines like melted gold. Now, you know when you look into a mirror you can see pictures of the things in front of it - your own face, the walls of the room, the furniture. That is because the mirror is so bright that it reflects these things; yet the mirror is not bright enough to reflect anything except what is there before it, such things as you can see with your eyes and touch with your hands. But the fire can do better than that, for it is a great deal brighter than the mirror, and it is so bright that it can reflect thoughts. So you must think of the pictures first, and then, if you know just how to look for them in the fire, you will find them reflected there, and after a little while you will be surprised at the wonderful things you will see."

"I don't know what you mean at all," said the child; "tell me what you can see in the fire now."

"Very well. Suppose, then, first, that you almost close your eyes, but not quite, so that you will not see the fire so plainly, and it will all run together and look dim and misty. When I look at it in that way it seems to me to be fire no more, but water. It is as if we were down under a broad, deep river, and could see all the mass of water slowly eddying and whirling and flowing on above us, with just the little glow and glimmer of brightness that come down from the daylight and the air above. But there is one little spot that is brighter, right in the middle of the fire, where you see that one little yellow flame all by itself. In my picture, it is like a big lump of pure gold, resting on a point of rock that stands straight up from the bottom of the river. It is really gold, and magic gold at that, for you know wonderful treasures often lie at the bottoms of rivers. One of the wonderful things about this gold is that, if anybody could have a ring made of it, he could compel everybody else to obey him and serve him, and could rule the whole world.

"Three forms I can see now moving backward and forward, and up and down, and around and around about the gold. Now they grow a little clearer. They are river nymphs, or something of the sort, and they are here to guard the gold, lest anybody should try to steal it. It would not be easy to steal, even if it had no guard, and knowing this has perhaps made these pretty keepers a little careless about it, so that now, instead of watching it very closely, they are swimming and diving and circling about, trying to catch one another, having the jolliest time in the world, and never thinking that there may be danger near."

"And you can see all those things in the fire?" said the little girl. "I can't see any of them. How do you see them?"

"Just as I told you at first, by thinking of them and then seeing the thoughts reflected there."

"Well, tell me some more."

"Look at that little dark spot under the fire. When I look at it in the way I have told you, it is the form of a dwarf. He is ugly and rough-looking, he is crooked, and he has a wicked face. He slips and tumbles slowly along, till he catches sight of the water nymphs, and they look so pretty and graceful and happy, as they chase one another about and up and down and around, that his cruel little eyes light up with pleasure, and he calls to them that he should like to come up and play with them too."

"Oh, now I don't believe any of it at all," said the child; "I thought just for a little while you might know how to see all those funny things in the fire, but you can't hear people talk in the fire."

"Oh, my dear child, you don't know very much about the fire if you think I can't see anything I want to in it, or hear anything I want to either. I tell you I can hear what this dwarf says, just as plainly as I can see him walk about. Still, if you don't believe any of it and don't care to know about the dwarf and the nymphs and the gold, perhaps you might better go and study your multiplication table, and I will find something else to do."

"Oh, but I do want to know about them. Please tell me some more. What do the nymphs say to the dwarf? Can you hear that too?"

"Of course I can hear it; they call to him to come up and play with them if he likes, and he clambers up over the rocks and trees to catch one of them after another, while they swim and glide away from him, and find it much better fun than chasing one another. It is good fun, no doubt, for the dwarf cannot swim like them, but only scrambles about in the most ridiculous way, with never any hope of catching one of them, except when she lets him come near her for a moment, to plague him by slipping away again quite out of his reach. At last he gets thoroughly tired and discouraged and angry, while the three sisters laugh at him and taunt him and chatter with one another, and have clearly enough forgotten all about the gold that they are supposed to be watching.

"But see now how much brighter the fire is getting. It makes me think that something must have happened up above the river. The sun must have risen, or something of that sort, for everything looks clearer and the gold shines out so bright and beautiful, that the blear-eyed dwarf himself sees it and forgets all about trying to catch water nymphs in wondering what it is. He asks the nymphs, and they tell him about the ring that could be made of it if only it could be stolen from them; but it is of no use for him to try, they say, because it is a part of the magic of the gold that it can never be stolen except by some one who loves nobody in the world and has sworn that he will never love anybody, and it is clear enough that the dwarf is in love with all three of them at this very minute. When such a strange treasure as this was to be guarded, it was no doubt very clever to set three such beautiful creatures as these to watch it, for if a thief were not in love already, it is a hundred to one that he would be before he got near enough to the gold to steal it.

"But the nymphs do not understand at all how much more a heartless little monster like this dwarf loves the glitter of gold than he could ever possibly love them. So, even while they are laughing at him, he is forgetting them completely, and then he swears a deep oath that as long as he lives he will never love any living thing. Now, if you can think of anything that anybody could do more wicked, more horrible, more cruel than that, you must know a great deal more about wicked and horrible things than you have any right to know. After that every kind of wrong is easy, and a little thing like stealing a lump of gold of the size of a bushel basket is a mere nothing. The dwarf scrambles up the point of rock again, while the nymphs, who think that he is still chasing them, swim far away from him, and he seizes the gold and plunges down to the bottom with it. The nymphs rush together again with a cry of horror and grief and fright, and in an instant everything is dark, as the flames of our fire suddenly drop down.

"But you see they fall only for a moment, and now, as they blaze up again, brighter than ever, I see another picture. It is on the hilltop above the river. The grass there is soft and fresh, the trees are cool and green, and the mellow light of morning is over them all. A light, white morning mist comes up from the river, and the sun, which has just risen from behind the purple hills, away off where the sky touches them, turns the mist into shifting and shimmering silver, so that it makes the whole scene look brighter instead of dimmer. On the hill across the river is a glorious sight. It is a castle, the grandest and most beautiful you ever saw. Its walls are thick and strong enough for a fortress, yet its towers and battlements look so light and graceful that you would think they might hold themselves up there in the air, or rest on the silver river mist, if there were no walls under them. As I look at the castle through the mist it seems half clear and solid and firm, and half wavering and dim, mysterious and magical, like a castle in a dream.

"There is something magical about it, for it was all built in one night by two giants, and they built it for the gods themselves. And now you must be prepared to meet some very fine company, for right here before us are the great Father and the great Mother of the gods, looking across the river at their splendid new home."

"Do you mean Jupiter and Juno?" the little girl asked.

"No, these are not Jupiter and Juno; and the other gods whom we shall see soon, if the fire burns right, are not the gods you know already, but they are a good deal like them in some ways. The Father of the Gods is full of joy at having such a glorious castle, and the Mother of the Gods is full of dread at the price that must be paid to the giants for building it. A terrible price indeed it is, as she does not hesitate to remind him, for the gods have promised to give the giants the beautiful Goddess of Love and Youth. It was a foolish and wicked promise for them to make, foolish because if they kept it they could never in the world get on without her, and wicked because they did not intend to keep it. The homes of the gods, like any other homes, would be dreary enough without the Goddess of Love, but it is worse than that, for she has a garden where apples grow for the gods to eat; it is eating these apples that makes the gods always young, and nobody but her knows how to care for them, so that if she goes away the gods will begin to grow old at once and will soon die."

"Were the apples like that - oh, what was it? you know the name of it - that the other gods used to eat?"

"Ambrosia? Yes, something like it, but not quite. You know the gods who ate ambrosia would live forever and are living still; we have seen some of them ourselves up among the stars. But these gods have to eat the apples often, and they must get them from the Goddess of Love. This is much the better story of the two, I think, because it shows us how gods and other people, as long as they keep love with them, will be always young, no matter how many years they may live; and how, if they let it go away from them, they will be old at once, no matter how few their years.

"All this the Father and the Mother of the Gods are talking over together now, and he tells her how the Fire God, who proposed the bargain in the first place, said that the price need never be paid and that he trusts the Fire God may yet find some way out of the trouble. Yet the giants must be made in some way to give up their price of themselves, for the Father of the Gods has the words of the promise cut upon his spear, and he cannot break a promise that he has once made. The Fire God has gone away now to search through the world for something that may be offered to the giants instead of the Goddess of Love. And now I see her come, running to the Father of the Gods for protection, and the other gods are here, to help her if they can, and the giants themselves have come to claim her for the building of the castle.

"Well, to be sure, they are all in a fine state of excitement. The giants are big, dreadful-looking fellows, with clubs made of the trunks of trees, and the poor goddess does not want to go with them in the least. All the other gods declare, too, that she shall not go with them, and the giants insist that she shall. The Thunder God is there and he has a wonderful hammer, a blow of which is like a stroke of lightning. He is about to strike the giants with it, and that, you may be sure, would settle the whole matter, big as they are, but the Father of the Gods will not let him harm them. He has promised, and whatever happens he cannot break his word.

"While everything is in this dreadful state, the Fire God comes back from his search. It is not a very cheering story that he has to tell. He has been through all the world, he says, and he has asked everywhere what there is that is as good for gods or giants, or anybody else, as the love of a woman, which makes those who have it always young. But the people in those days knew more than a good many of the people in these days, and everywhere they laughed at him and told him that he might as well give up his search, for he would never find what he sought."

"What do you mean by 'the people in those days'?" the child asked; "I thought you said you could see them right here in the fire now."

"So I can, but it is the beauty of these pictures in the fire that I can see things that happened years ago, thousands of years ago, if I like, just as well as things that happen now, and perhaps a little better. So you see the Fire God has not had very good luck, but as he was coming back, he says, he passed near where the river nymphs were, and they called to him, telling him that their beautiful gold had been stolen, and begging him to ask the Father of the Gods to get it back for them. They told him, too, about the wicked dwarf who stole it, and how, before he could steal it, he had to swear never again, as long as he lived, to love anybody or anything. The Fire God seems to have heard about the dwarf somewhere else, too, for he says that he has already made the magic ring out of the gold, that by the help of the ring he has compelled all the other dwarfs to obey him and serve him, and has piled up such a treasure of gold and jewels as was never seen before; and finally, that, if the gods are not careful, the dwarf will soon rule over them and the whole world besides.

"So it seems that there is one person in the world who has found something which he thinks is worth more than love. And there are at least two others who are as foolish as he, though they may not be quite so wicked. And these are the giants, for when they hear the Fire God tell of the wonderful treasure that the dwarf has heaped together, they say to the gods that they think the dwarf is quite right, they would rather have all that gold than the love of any woman, and, if the gods will get it for them, they may keep their Goddess of Love and Youth. The Father of the Gods hesitates; how can he get the treasure? he asks.

"'You can find some way to get it, if you like,' the giants reply.

"'I will not get it for you; you shall not have it,' says the Father of the Gods.

"'Then we will hold to our first bargain,' they answer, 'and take your Love Goddess with us. To-night we will bring her back; if you have the treasure ready for us, then you may keep her; if not, then you have lost her forever.' And they seize her and stride away, dragging her with them, while the gods look on in grief and fear. And well they may fear at the change that comes as soon as the beautiful goddess is gone. You can see the change yourself in the fire. If it did not fit the story that I am finding in it so well, I should say that the fire needed more wood, for it seems almost out; see how the blackened sticks are smouldering and smoking, with scarcely any bright flames at all. The smoke is spreading like an ugly gray cloud over everything; the trees and the flowers droop; the sky is dull and the grass is dingy; the castle looks grim and heavy, and no longer bright and graceful; the faces of the gods themselves grow pale and haggard; they feel that they are suddenly older. They have not eaten the apples of youth to-day, and nobody can get them but the one goddess who has gone. They know that they will grow older every hour and will soon die if they do not get her back, and the only way is to find the dwarf's treasure for the giants.

"'Come quickly,' says the Father of the Gods, 'and let us get this treasure; let us hasten down under the ground where the dwarfs live, for we must have it to-night, when the giants come.'

"There, where the dirty yellow smoke is pouring out between the sticks of wood at the top of the pile, I see a crevice in the rocks. The Father of the Gods and the Fire God go down into it, and the smoke comes thicker and blacker, and hides everything but those two, and I see them climbing down and down over the rough, sharp rocks, toward the caverns of the dwarfs, while the little tongues of flame shoot out at them from the fissures, as if they were trying to catch and burn and sting them, just as they shoot out from between the black, charred sticks here before our eyes.

"It is a deep, dark cave that I see now, with little spots of light here and there, like forges, and there is the sound of anvils. The dwarfs live here, and they are all working hard, as they must now, for the dwarf who stole the gold and made the ring from it. I see him too, and he is scolding and beating another dwarf, who is his brother. It is all about a piece of fine metal work that he has set his brother to do, and now the brother wants to keep what he has made. But he drops it on the ground and the dwarf king, for a king he really is now, picks it up and claps it on his head. It is a helmet, made of delicate rings of steel linked together. It is a magic helmet, and anybody who wears it can disappear from sight whenever he likes, or can take any shape he chooses. In a minute the dwarf is no more to be seen, and in his place there is only a cloud of smoke. But he can still beat his brother, and presently he leaves him whining and crying on the ground, and the cloud floats away.

"You are not to suppose because this dwarf is treated in this cruel way that he is any better than his brother who beats him. One of them is just as wicked as the other, and he deserves all he gets. So here, lying upon the ground and groaning, the two gods find him, as they come down into the cave. 'What is the matter?' they ask, and he tells them about the magic helmet. Then back comes the other dwarf, who wears the helmet and the ring, driving before him a crowd of his fellows, all laden down with gold and gems, and they throw them in a pile. They are so rich and dazzling, and there is such a quantity of them that the fire actually burns brighter there in the corner where they have heaped them up. The dwarf drives all his workmen away, and then sulkily asks the gods what they want here, for with his ring and his helmet he thinks that he is just as good as any of the gods.

"The Fire God tells him that they have heard so much about his great wealth that they have come to see it, and now they find his treasure greater and finer than anything they ever saw before. At that the dwarf is flattered and begins to boast. 'This that you see is nothing,' he says; 'I shall soon have much more, and by the magic of my ring I mean to rule the whole world and you gods too.'

"'But suppose,' says the Fire God, 'that some one should steal the ring from you while you were asleep?'

"'That shows how little you know about it,' the dwarf answers. 'Why, do you see this magic helmet of mine? With this I can make myself invisible, or I can take any form I like, and so nobody can find me while I am asleep to steal the ring.'

"'Oh, now you are telling us too big a story,' says the Fire God; 'it is nonsense to say you can take any form you like, helmet or no helmet; you can't expect us to believe that.'

"At this the dwarf begins to get a little angry; 'I tell you I can,' he cries; 'I will prove it to you; I can change myself into anything; what shall it be?'

"'Oh, whatever you like,' says the Fire God, 'only let it be something big and horrible to show just how much you can do.'

"So, to show what he can do, in a second the dwarf changes himself into a horrible dragon, with slimy scales and a writhing tail, and eyes and jaws that look as wicked as the dwarf himself, and twice as savage. The Fire God pretends to be dreadfully frightened, and when the dwarf comes back to his own shape again he says: 'That was very good, but that does not seem so hard, after all. Now, the way for you to hide, it seems to me, would be to make yourself very small, so that you could slip into a crack in the rocks. You can puff yourself up like a dragon, of course, but can you make yourself small as easily? Oh, no, I cannot believe that.'

"'I can be anything, anything, I tell you,' the dwarf cries, getting still more angry; 'I will be as small as you like,' and in another second he has changed himself into a toad, not much bigger than your hand, as slimy as ever, looking still just as wicked as the dwarf himself, and almost as ugly.

"'Now is the time - quick!' cries the Fire God, and in an instant the Father of the Gods stamps his foot upon the toad and has him fast. The Fire God stoops and pulls the magic helmet off the toad's head, and instantly he is the dwarf again, but he is still firmly held under the god's foot, and they tie him with cords and drag him away with them, up among the rocks from which they came."

"That is just the way Puss in Boots caught the ogre, when he turned himself into a mouse," said the little girl.

"Yes, to be sure it is, but you know there are only a very few stories in the world, any way, and we cannot find new ones. The most we can ever do is to tell the old ones over in different ways, and after all it is better so, for old things are better than new almost always, as you will find when you get a little older yourself. But now, with the fire burning up a little better to help me, we are back above ground. Let us put on more wood and see if we cannot make it better yet. We are just where we were before, on the hill by the river and the castle of the gods. And back now come the two gods from under the ground, dragging the dwarf with them.

'And what will you give us now,' they cry, 'if we will untie you and let you go?'

"'What must I give you?' he asks.

"'You must give us the whole of your treasure,' they answer; 'we will not let you go for anything less.'

"That seems a large price, but the dwarf is as crafty as he is wicked, though his craft seldom does him much good, and he thinks that even if he gives up all his treasure he can soon pile up as much more, with the help of the ring. So, by the power of the ring, he calls the dwarfs to bring him the treasure, and up they come with it, out of the cleft of the rocks, and they pile it in a great, glittering heap just there where the new fire is beginning to burn so bright. 'There is the gold,' cries the dwarf, 'let me go.'

"'Not yet,' says the Father of the Gods; 'give us your ring first, that belongs to the treasure.'

"At that the dwarf screams and struggles and writhes and curses the gods, but it is all of no use; the Father of the Gods tears the ring from his finger, and then they untie him and tell him to take himself off where he will. And now, as he goes, he lays a terrible curse on the ring. To every one who shall ever gain it, he swears, shall come ill luck, misfortune, sorrow, terror, and death; let him rule the world if he will, never shall he be happy; everyone shall long for the ring, and to him who gets it, it shall bring misery and ruin. Truly the dwarf has gained little by stealing the gold from the river nymphs, but the gods have done wrong as well in stealing it from him, and they are doing wrong still in not giving it back to the nymphs; so they must suffer too.

"But it is not yet time for that, for now, as the fire burns up, the whole picture grows brighter again. That is because the giants are bringing back the Goddess of Love and Youth, to see if the treasure is ready for them. The trees lift up their branches again and the happy sunlight pours down through them; the flowers open their eyes to see it; the sky is clear and bright, and the grass is again fresh; while the faces of the gods, who run to meet their sister, look young and happy as before. Only the castle is still hidden by the shining silver river mist. The giants have come near. 'Is the ransom ready for us?' they cry.

"'There is your treasure.' says the Father of the Gods, 'take it and be gone.'

"'We must see that it is enough first,' they answer; 'our treasure must be as much as your goddess, so you must pile it up before her till she is quite hidden by it; then we will take it, and you shall have her back.'

"They heap up the gold and the jewels before the goddess, higher and higher, till everything is gone from the old pile to the new one. Then one of the giants looks over it and still sees the gold of her hair above the gold of the treasure. 'Give me that helmet that you carry,' he says to the Fire God, 'to put on the top.' and he gives it. Now the other giant peeps through a chink in the pile and sees one of her eyes. 'Quick,' he cries to the Father of the Gods, 'give me that ring you wear to stop this chink.'

"'No,' says the Father of the Gods, 'you shall not have that; it is the ring that gives the power to rule the world, and I will keep it.'

"' Very well, then,' say the giants, 'we will have no more to do with you, and we will take the goddess back with us.'

"All the gods stand terrified and pale. Will their great father let the Goddess of Love be taken from them again, and must they all grow old and die, that he may keep this ring? Everything grows dark again, as our fire here drops down; only there is that pale blue flame that gives no light, away at the back of the hearth. And now, right in the pale blue flame, rises the form of a woman out of the ground. It is the Earth Goddess, the wisest woman in the world, who knows all that ever was, all that is, and all that ever shall be. She speaks to the Father of the Gods and tells him to give the ring to the giants, for the curse that the dwarf has laid upon it will surely destroy him who keeps it. Then she sinks out of sight, and the Father of the Gods takes from his finger the ring, and gives it.

"And even while the giants are stowing the treasure in a sack to carry it away, they fall to quarrelling about how it shall be divided, and one of them strikes the other a terrible blow with his club which lays him dead upon the ground. Then he strides away with the treasure, leaving the gods filled with horror at the first fatal work done by the curse of the ring.

"Yet only for a moment; their grand new castle is ready for them now. High up upon a rock stands the Thunder God. He swings his hammer and the black clouds roll around him. The thunder mutters, and lightning flames flash out from the dark vapors. The fire flickers and blazes up again, the clouds part and melt away, and all is light at last. A rainbow reaches across the river from shore to shore, and the gods slowly walk across upon it toward their castle. Up from the river, far below them, comes a sad cry of the nymphs, begging the gods to give them back their gold. But the gods do not heed it. They rest upon the rainbow, gazing only at their castle, as it stands before them, stately, graceful, radiant, and rosy in the warm glow of the sunset."

"And did you really, really see it all in the fire?" the little girl asked, after she had thought it all over for a few minutes. "It sounds just as if it was a story you had read in a book."

"Well, perhaps I may have seen something, or heard something, or read something of the kind somewhere," I replied, "but you know I told you at first that you must think of the pictures before you could see them reflected in the fire."

The little girl sat still and thought about it again for a time. "I don't believe you saw any pictures in the fire at all," she said at last.

THE DAUGHTER OF THE GOD

"If you say you can see all those things in the fire," said the little girl, with an air of doubt not yet quite overcome, "I suppose I shall have to believe it, but I don't see how. I try to think of them the way you said, but I don't see them in the fire a bit. Can you see them all the time?"

"It makes a good deal of difference how I feel about it," I answered, "and a little difference how the fire burns. To-night, you see, the fire does not burn quite as it usually does. It is cold out of doors, and there is a wind that comes in gusts and blows different ways. It gives the fire a good draught, and on the whole it burns rather fiercely, but when the wind goes down the fire goes down a little too, and when the wind changes it blows a puff of smoke down the chimney now and then. Altogether it is not a well-behaved fire at all, and I am afraid if we try to see things in it, some of them will be rather rough and rude, and none of them very cheerful. Still, if you would like to try - "

"Oh, do try," the child said, "I like nice gloomy things."

"Very well. Just now the fire is so fierce and hot that it seems to me nothing less than a house on fire. It is a house that stands all alone in the woods. Before it was set on fire a boy and a girl lived there. Neither of them had any mother, but the boy's father lived with them and took care of them, going out hunting and leaving the boy and the girl together, till the boy was old enough to go hunting with him, and then the girl was left alone. They were very happy there together, all three of them, and the father always thought that the girl would sometime grow up and be his son's wife. But now, while they are hunting, a robber has come and has burned the house, and he takes the girl with him and carries her off to his own house, far away among the mountains.

"After this it is not so pleasant roaming the woods and hunting all day, with no house to go back to and no greeting of a bright face in the evening. To make it still worse, one day, while they are hunting, the poor boy loses sight of his father and never finds him again. So now he is quite alone, but he still lives in the woods in the old way till he grows to be a tall, strong, handsome young man. Perhaps he is all the stronger and the better fighter because the most of his enemies, and his friends too, for that matter, have been wild beasts. That he has had one good enemy I know, because the coat that he wears is the skin of a bear.

"And all this time the girl has been kept a prisoner at the house of the robber, and she has grown up as well, now, to be a tall, beautiful woman. At times, no doubt, the robber has treated her well enough, and at times, I am afraid, not so well. But always he has urged her and has tried to make her promise to be his wife, and now, after all these years, at last she has promised. She has never forgotten the brave boy whom she used to love, but the robber has told her that he is dead, and finally she has come to believe it and has no more any hope of ever being happy.

"I am looking right into the robber's house now. It is a strange house, for right in the middle of it stands a large tree, which grows up through the roof and spreads its branches over the house. And more wonderful still, there is a sword sticking in this tree, up to the hilt. Perhaps I might better tell you something about this sword before we go any farther. Do you remember the gold that was stolen from the river nymphs, the other night, when we were watching the fire, and the magic ring that the dwarf made of it? Of course you do, and you remember too how the Father of the Gods got it and paid it to the giants for building his castle, and would not give it back to the river nymphs, and how one of the giants killed the other and kept all the treasure. Well, the Father of the Gods has been learning and thinking a good deal since then, and he has begun to see what a great wrong he did when he put the gold to his own uses, instead of giving it back to the nymphs. It is no light punishment that falls on gods when they do wrong, and he sees that for this sin he and all the other gods who live with him in his castle must at last be destroyed utterly. Yet he still hopes to save them if only the gold, or at least the ring, can be given back again to the nymphs.

"Now, the giant who took all the treasure carried it away to a deep cave in the side of a mountain, and then, by the help of the magic helmet, he changed himself into a horrible, fierce, fiery, poisonous dragon, so that he might stay in the cave and guard it. And there he has stayed guarding it ever since. You will see at once that the treasure never would do him any good in that way, but giants are usually stupid, and he could not think of anything better to do with it. A boy who has a penny and knows enough to buy a penny whistle with it is richer than this dragon giant. Yet he guards the treasure pretty well, and the Father of the Gods cannot take it away from him, and cannot help anybody else to take it away from him, because he paid it to him for the castle, and to touch it now would be to break his promise. Yet he wishes that somebody, without his help, would kill the dragon and give the gold back to its real owners. This would not really do him any good, for his own old sin would still be just as great, and he knows it; yet he has a strange kind of hope that it may somehow help him. But the dragon is so big and fierce and fiery and poisonous, that nobody could ever hope to kill him except the very greatest of heroes, and one who simply did not know what fear meant. Even such a hero might have a good deal of trouble about it, if he did not have a sword that was just as keen and strong, just as sharp and firm and true as himself. So, that he may not want for such a good blade, the Father of the Gods has made a magic sword. No one but a god could make a sword like this, and he has driven it up to the hilt into the great tree in the robber's house. It is quite safe there, for the magic of it is that nobody but the bravest, strongest, truest hero living can ever draw it out, but for him it will be easy. There are some things besides drawing swords out of trees which can be done easily by men who are brave and strong and true, and which no other man can do at all.

"All this time I have been looking into the robber's house. There is a storm outside, worse than the wind that is troubling our fire. It howls above the house, and tears at the branches of the tree, till even the great trunk shivers and trembles and makes the roof creak and groan. Suddenly the door is burst open, and in, out of the storm, rushes a man, and falls before the fire as if he were so weary that he could move no more. Then from another room of the house comes the woman who has promised to be the robber's wife, the girl who once lived in the house that the robber burned. When she sees the stranger lying before the fire, she lifts him up and brings him a big drinking-horn, and tells him to stay and rest till the robber comes home. Then he looks at her, and she seems to him the kindest, the sweetest, and the loveliest woman he has ever seen.

"Soon the robber comes home, and he asks the stranger what he is and how he came here. Then the stranger tells him all the story that I have told you of the burning of the house where he lived with his father, and how since then he has wandered the woods and has fought with the wild beasts and with his enemies. As soon as he tells that, the woman knows that the boy whom she used to love so long ago is not dead, but is sitting here before her, and the hope comes to her that he may take her away from this place, so that she may not have to be married to the robber. Then she asks the stranger why he is unarmed, and he says that he fought to rescue a woman from her enemies; he killed some of them, but the others were so many that they broke his spear and his shield, and he had to save himself from them, and so it was that he came to this house.

"At this the robber grows red and pale with anger. He has heard of the fight, and the men who were killed were his friends. 'Stay here to-night,' he says; 'while you are in my house I cannot harm you, but to-morrow you must go out and fight with me for killing my friends.'

"The robber and the woman have gone away and the

stranger is left alone. Sad and gloomy enough are his thoughts, for to-morrow he must fight with the robber, and he has no sword, no spear, no shield. The fire before him dies down, as our fire dies down too, for the moment, and as all his hope grows darker and colder. And then, just as his life and the world and the future seem blackest, the woman comes back. Why should her coming bring him hope? He could not tell, perhaps, yet her very presence cheers him; misfortune and death seem not so near when she is by, and not so terrible, even should they come. He may not know why it is, but I know, and so do you.

"She hastens to him and shows him the sword in the tree. She tells him of its magic; he must be the hero to draw it out, she says, and then, in the fight to-morrow, he must overcome his enemy and give her revenge for all she had suffered from him. And how gladly he will do her bidding! He seizes the sword and draws it quickly out of the tree, while her eyes gaze at him and are filled with joy. The hero has come - her hero. He holds the wonderful magic sword in his hand, but only for a moment he looks upon its long, gleaming, beautiful blade. Then he turns to her again. They twine their arms about each other and together they leave this hateful house. And now, of a sudden, it is as if their two hearts were all the world, as indeed they are, to each other, for all around them the storm was stilled; the winter is gone and it is spring; the peaceful moonlight fills the happy woods with a soft glory; sweet airs breathe tenderly on them and on the flowers in their path; quiet voices speak to them out of the budding trees; and so together they are gone into the forest.

"The Father of the Gods has done more than I have

told you yet to guard against the end which he knows must come, in spite of all that he can do. He has fancied that his castle might be safer if he were to fill it with strong warriors to fight for him in any need. Therefore, wherever battles are fought he sends his nine daughters to choose the bravest of the men who are killed and to bring them to his castle. Each of these daughters has a horse which flies through the air faster than any bird. When the fallen heroes have come thus to the halls of the gods, they are brought to life and their wounds are healed by means that the gods know how to use, and they live there, feasting day after day with other heroes. And lest they should forget their old skill and bravery in fighting, every day they have a battle and many of them are killed and chopped to pieces by the others' swords, but at sunset they are all alive and well again, and they go back together to their feast in the halls of the gods.

"It is one of these daughters of the god, one of these choosers of heroes, whom I see before me now. I wish that I could make you see her. She is more than a beautiful woman, and also she is less. She is tall and her form is strong, yet light and buoyant. She is dressed all in armor, and she has a spear and a shield which gleams and glistens like a beacon-light for an army. She herself, as I see her here, is as graceful and as full of warm life as a flame of the fire, the same hot glow stirs her heart and moves her to the same eager, free action. Her face is as clear and pure as the fire itself, and almost as radiant as her silver shield, while the gold of her hair breaking from under the light of her helmet, outshines them all. Beating under her bosom, thrilling through her form, glowing in her cheeks, and beaming from her eyes, is the joy of life and strength and beauty. Yet where is the tenderness that one would seek in a woman's eyes? A glad light shines in hers, but it is not softened by any kindly ray of gentleness or mercy. Where is the sweetness of a woman's lips? Hers are calm and beautiful, but they tempt no more than a stain of blood upon the snow. What is there in her face that could melt into a woman's compassion and pity? Her face is not cruel, not unkind, only still, stern, and placid as marble. She is not a woman, you know; only a goddess - a war goddess.

"Just now the Father of the Gods is telling his daughter of the fight that is to come between the robber and the hero who won the sword, and he commands her to help the hero to win. She is delighted at this, for she loves all brave, true heroes as he does, but she has scarcely left her father when the Mother of the Gods comes, riding furiously through the air in a chariot drawn by two rams. She has heard of the fight too, and she takes quite a different view of it. 'This man whom you would save and help,' she says, 'has taken the woman away from the man whose wife she promised to be. Is that all you care for a promise? He must be punished; you must help his enemy to kill him.'

"You see she cares nothing at all about heroes, but to her a promise is a promise. And the Father of the Gods himself is very particular about promises, as you must remember, so he is forced to say that he will not help the hero. But that is not enough for her; he must command his daughter not to help him. She shall not, he says, but that is not enough; he must help his enemy and see that he wins. This is hard for the Father of the Gods, for he loves the hero, and if he is left to himself he must win, with his magic sword, yet he cannot choose; the promise has been broken, and he gives his word that the hero shall die.

"The Father of the Gods is left alone, and again his daughter comes to him. He tells her sadly that she must help the robber in the fight, and that the hero must die. She is as sad as he at this command, for all that she ever wishes is to do what he would have her do, and she knows that, though he says that the hero must die, yet he would have him live. But his word is given, and, full of sorrow, the god and his daughter part. And now comes the hero himself, with his bride. She is fearful of what may befall him in the fight, and would have him flee farther away. He will not do that, and he tries to cheer her, till she faints and sinks down at his feet. Then, beautiful and sad, but still calm, stern, and placid, the Daughter of the God stands before him.

"'Soon,' she says to him, 'you must come with me to the castle of the gods. There the Father of the Gods will welcome you, there your own father, whom you lost so long ago, waits for you, there you will fight and feast with heroes, and the daughters of the god will serve you.'

"'And shall this woman here,' he asks, 'whom I love, go with me and with you there?'

"'No,' she answers, 'this woman cannot go.'

"'Then I will not go,' he replies; 'gladly I would stand before the Father of the Gods, gladly I would see my own father again and the heroes and the daughters of the god, but not without her; I will not go with you; leave us here.'

"If the daughter of the god were a woman she would

understand all this, but now it would make her impatient, if anything could. She cannot know and cannot feel why this man, who has had only trouble and ill luck all his life, should choose to stay and wait for more trouble and ill luck with this one poor woman who lies at their feet, fainting and knowing not even that she is alive, rather than to sit and feast with gods and heroes. How little a war goddess can really know about brave men!

"Yet she does know that her father, whose wishes are her own, wishes this woman to live, and that she will be in danger after her hero has left her; so she tells him that he may leave his bride with her and she will protect her. But the man is still more unreasonable. He says that she is cruel and hard-hearted. That is unjust, for she is not cruel. He says too that the woman shall die rather than be left with her. If he must die, he will kill the woman, too, and he is about to do it, when the Daughter of the God holds his hand. She thinks only now of how much her father longs that this man may live; she resolves that in spite of the command she will save him; she tells him that he shall have her help in the fight, and she leaves him, just as there comes a noise and a shout of the robber with his men and his dogs hunting for the hero to kill him.

"See how the black smoke is driven down the chimney by the changing gusts of wind. It is like dark clouds gathering over the sky and dropping down upon the mountain, so that it is hard to see anything at all. The fire goes down, too, and its flames dart and flicker in sudden, angry flashes. Some of them are like lightning, brightening the whole scene for an instant, and then I can see the hero and the robber in their fight, springing and thrusting and striking at each other so that it seems as if they must both be killed a dozen times over. Again in the sparkle of the fire I see the gleaming of the magic sword, as the hero whirls it above his head and strikes at his enemy. Then comes a flare of flame that shines from the shield of the Daughter of the God, as she throws it over the hero to protect and save him. It is all in vain, for there comes a hot, red glow in which for an instant all the rest is lost, and now, in the midst of it stands the Father of the Gods himself. The daughter falls back helpless before him, and he stretches his spear toward the hero. The magic sword falls upon the spear and is shivered to pieces. Nothing indeed could shatter that blade but the spear of the god who made it, but with that spear to help him the robber springs upon his enemy and his sword is through his heart, and he is fallen.

"The Daughter of the God has come back to where the woman lay, she has lifted her from the ground and has laid her across her horse's saddle as if she were dead; she leaps upon his back and they are galloping away like the wind. The Father of the Gods has avenged the broken promise; he has killed the hero whom he loved, and now he turns for one moment toward the robber whom he has helped to win the fight. Only once the god waves his hand toward him and the robber falls dead; he will fight and kill brave men no more. But a harder task than all is to come for the Father of the Gods; how shall he deal with his own daughter, who has disobeyed him?

"The fire is burning a little better now, but it does not yet seem to be quite on good terms with the wind outside. The smoke is going up again instead of down, and that is an improvement. It rises in sudden puffs and flurries, like clouds flying across the sky after a storm.

The shadows of the clouds fall upon a mountain height, a rugged, rocky, wild, beautiful place, where the daughters of the god are meeting to ride home together with the heroes they have brought from some field of battle. Now and then, as the quick flames leap up into the smoke, I can see another and another coming, riding on her flying horse, racing with the driving wind and the hurrying clouds, each with her warrior lying before her across her saddle, and so alighting here and joining her sisters. They are all here at last except the one Daughter of the God whom we have seen before, and now she comes, but she brings no warrior across her saddle, only the poor woman with whom she fled from the fight.

"She tells her sisters how she has disobeyed their father, and she begs them to protect her and the woman against his anger. They dare not help her; never has one of them done anything that was not his will. What can she do? He is coming in pursuit of her; sooner or later he must find her, but she may at least save the woman. She bids her flee alone while she waits with her sisters for her father and her punishment to come. Far away, she tells her, there is a deep forest, and in the forest is a cave where the horrible dragon that was once the giant keeps and guards his treasure. So much does the Father of the Gods dread the curse that the wicked dwarf laid upon the ring, and the doom which he knows is coming to himself because of his own sin, that he never wanders there. To this forest she must go, and there she may find a refuge. The Daughter of the God gives the woman the fragments of the broken magic sword, which she has brought with her from the field of the fight, and bids her go.

"And now, with angry lightnings flashing all around

him, comes the Father of the Gods. Never before has he been shaken by such a storm as this. His daughter whom he loved more than all the others, has disobeyed him. Never before has she done anything but that which it was his will that she should do. Now she has known his will, she has heard his command, and she has broken it. She stands before him, sorrowful, but still calm, stern, and placid, and asks what is to be her punishment. She has brought her doom upon herself, he answers, and now she must be a war goddess no more, but only a woman. He must kiss her once, and all the strength and the valor and the pride of the goddess will be gone. Then she will sink to sleep, and here on this rocky mountain height she must lie till some man comes and awakes her, and she must be a woman only and his wife.

"Very dreadful this seems to the poor war goddess, but it is because she has never been a woman, and does not know much about women. To me it does not seem dreadful at all. It is much better and sweeter and nobler, I believe, to be the best that a woman can be than the strongest and greatest and proudest that a goddess can be. And I hope you will always remember what we see here in the fire to-night, and if you ever feel that there is any danger of your being a goddess, or if anybody ever tells you that you are one, then let somebody kiss you and make you a woman.

"But to one who has so long been used to wearing armor and riding through the air, and choosing the bravest of the fallen heroes, and bearing them to the castle of the gods, the change may well seem hard to suffer at first. So the Daughter of the God thinks that no heavier punishment could have been found for her. Her sisters think so, too, and they beg their father to have mercy on her, but he sternly bids them be silent and to leave him. Now the Daughter of the God tells him how she tried to do what he would have her do; she knew that he loved the hero and hated the robber, and that his command to her was given unwillingly; she hoped to gain for him the wish of his heart, in spite of his words, and she threw her shield over the hero.

"It is useless; he cannot stay her punishment now, but his anger is all gone and he is filled with sorrow like her own. He loves her still, more than any other daughter, and now he will never have her beside him in the halls of the gods again, never again see her ride to the battle, never see her return with brave men to guard his house, never again speak to her as he could to no other, and tell her all that is in his heart, never again see her glad, deep, answering eyes look into his, full of sympathy and help. One thing yet she begs: if all that they have been to each other, the god and his daughter, must be no more, if she must sleep and wait here for an unknown husband to wake her, she prays him to set some guard around her, a wall of fire, that no one but a brave man, the bravest of men, may win her for his bride.

"Yes, he will do this; she shall be shut in by fire and none shall ever come to her but the bravest of heroes, one who knows no fear at all. No one who fears even his own terrible spear, that spear which broke the magic sword that he himself had made, shall ever awake her who was his daughter, and now is to be his daughter no more. He draws her to him for one last time; he kisses her lips and they are silent; he kisses her eyes and they close. He lays her on a bank of soft moss; he closes her helmet and covers her with her shield. Near by her horse lies upon the ground asleep too; the flowers among the grass and in the crevices of the rocks droop their drowsy heads; the winds as they pass make no noise. He touches the point of his spear to the ground. Instantly the fire springs up; it makes a fierce, raging ring around the rock; surely only one who knows no fear can ever pass it. The Father of the Gods is gone. Now we can see nothing but the fire streaming up and exulting in its life and its hot defiance of all but the bravest; but there in the midst of it lies the Daughter of the God, asleep till her lover shall call her with a kiss to come with him and be a woman."

The little girl's mother had come into the room and had heard the last of the story. "Isn't it time," she said, "that the daughter of somebody else was asleep, too, if she wants to grow to be a woman?"

"It is late," I had to admit. "Well, the Daughter of the God is safe for the present. Perhaps some other time, when we have a better-behaved fire, we may see something of the lover."

THE HERO WHO KNEW NO FEAR

"Don't you think the fire is very good to-night?" the little girl asked.

"Yes, it is certainly very good indeed," I admitted.

"I should think," she said, "that anybody that could see things in fires might see very nice things in this one."

When she who might command deigns thus delicately to make a mere suggestion, it is the part both of chivalry and of loyalty to obey. I should feel that having my head chopped off was altogether too good for me if I hesitated at such a time. "Come," I said, "and let us see what the fire really looks like. What does it look like to you?"

"Oh, it doesn't look like anything at all to me, only just the fire. What does it to you?"

"It looks like a fire to me too, but it is the fire of a smith's forge. The place where it is looks half like a room and half like a cavern. It is all of rocks, but there is the forge and there are the chimney and the anvil and the bellows and all sorts of smith's tools."

"You can see things all around the fire, just the same as in it, can't you?" said the child.

"Oh, to be sure; when I want to see these things that make themselves into stories, I can see them almost anywhere, only I think the fire is a particularly good place. And who do you think is working at the forge? It is an ugly little dwarf, the very one whom we saw the other night, who made the magic helmet, the brother of the one who stole the treasure from the river nymphs. You remember he was a clever smith, else he never could have made that wonderful helmet. Now he is at work here trying to make a sword. And he does make a sword too, but he does not seem pleased with it when it is finished, and he leaves off his work and sits down, with a very dissatisfied, sulky, ugly look in his face.

"It would be hard for anybody to look more unlike the dwarf than the person I see now coming into the cave. He is a boy, or perhaps he would rather be called a young man, and I shall be glad to call him whatever he likes. He is dressed in skins and wears a little silver horn at his side. If the dwarf is short and ugly, he is tall and handsome; if the dwarf's face has a scowl of wicked hatred and cunning, his has a smile that beams with kindliness and candor; if the dwarf is old and crooked and rough and hairy, he is young and straight and graceful and fair. In short, you surely never saw a young man who looked more free, happy, generous, noble, strong, and bold than he. It makes one more good-humored to look at him, and the sunlight follows him straight into the cave. Something else follows him too, for he is leading a big brown bear by a cord twisted around its neck. He sends the bear at the dwarf, who screams and runs away in terror. The young man seems to have caught the bear in the woods just to frighten the dwarf, and he lets it go again when the dwarf tells him that the sword is finished and ready for him. He takes the sword and looks at it scornfully. It is good for nothing, he says. He strikes it upon the anvil and breaks it into a dozen pieces. He is a little particular about his swords; he does not like them unless he can chop anvils with them.

"Before we try to see any more, perhaps I ought to tell you something about this wonderful youth and why he lives here in the cave with the dwarf. He was born here. This is the forest where the treasure is hidden that was paid to the giants for building the castle of the gods. It is guarded, as you know, by the giant who killed his brother so that he might have the whole of it, and he has changed himself into a horrible dragon, by the magic helmet, so that he may guard it better. The young man's mother was the woman whom the Daughter of the God sent away into this forest to save her from the anger of the Father of the Gods, as you remember. She took refuge here in the dwarf's cave and she died soon after her son was born, and then the dwarf kept the boy and brought him up. But it was not because he cared for him at all or had the least kindly feeling for anybody. It was just because he wanted, as so many others wanted, that rich treasure and the magic helmet and the magic ring with the curse upon it.

"Now, you see, the boy's mother gave him the pieces of the broken magic sword and told him to keep them for the boy. He knew something about the sword and so he got it into his head that this was the very sword that would sometime kill that dragon. And since this boy was to have the sword, he thought, too, that he might very likely grow up to be the man who would kill the dragon. Do you see, then, why he has kept him and fed him and brought him up so carefully? It was just because he was so cunning and cruel and selfish that he took good care of the boy. He knew very well that he himself would never dare to go near enough to that dragon for it to breathe on him, but he thought: 'Some day I will give this boy the magic sword and make him go and kill the monster with it, and then I will kill him and get all the treasure, with the helmet and the ring, and then I shall be the ruler of all the dwarfs, of men, of the gods themselves, and of the whole world.'

"So the baby that the dwarf took and tended at first has grown to be this noble, brave, generous young man, and he hates the dwarf as anyone as good and strong as he must hate anything so cowardly and mean and wicked. All these years the dwarf has never told him anything about his mother or how he came to be living with him here in the cave. But now of a sudden the young man asks the dwarf some questions and shows that he means to treat him very roughly if he does not answer them. So the dwarf tells him a little of what I have told you, and to prove that what he says about his mother is true he shows him the pieces of the broken sword.

"The young man gets interested in these at once, you may be sure. 'That was a good sword,' he cries; 'that is the sword I must have; mend it for me, dwarf, and mend it quickly. I will go into the forest, and, if it is not done when I come back, you shall be sorry that you worked so badly.'

"Then away he goes to play with the bears, perhaps, in the forest. Now you can be quite sure that the dwarf has not kept that broken sword all these years without ever trying to mend it. He has tried many times, and he can no more put the pieces together than he can look as handsome as the fiery youth who has just left him here frightened half to death. So he simply sits down and lets himself get more frightened till he looks up and finds that he has a visitor.

"The visitor is a tall old man whom he does not know, but I know him; he is the Father of the Gods. He asks the dwarf to let him sit down and rest, but the dwarf is even more ill-natured than usual and bids him go away and not trouble him. The Father of the Gods replies that he might perhaps tell the dwarf something that would be of use to him if he would let him stay. Now you see what a good chance this would be for the dwarf to ask how to mend the broken sword, but he is so cross and surly that he thinks of nothing but how to be as disagreeable as possible, so he says that he knows all that he needs to know and does not care to learn from anybody. But the Father of the Gods persists; he will give the dwarf his head, he says, if he cannot answer any three questions that he may ask him. This pleases the dwarf, for he thinks it would be a pleasure to him to cut off somebody's head. 'What people, then,' he asks for his first question, 'live under the ground?'

"'The dwarfs,' says the stranger; 'one of them had a ring once, by which he ruled all the others.'

"'And what people,' asks the dwarf, 'live upon the mountains?'

"'The giants; one of them, in the form of a dragon, has the ring now.'

"'And who live up among the clouds?'

"'The gods,' says the stranger, 'and the Father of the Gods has a spear with which he rules the world.'

"As he says that, he lets the end of the spear which he carries drop upon the ground and instantly there is a peal of thunder.

"'Now,' says the stranger, 'as I have saved my head, you must pledge me yours to answer the three questions which I shall ask. Who is the strongest of heroes whom the Father of the Gods loves?'

"The dwarf answers that he thinks it must be the son of the woman who died long ago in the forest, who will kill the dragon and win the treasure. This is a good answer, and the stranger asks again: 'What sword must he use to kill the dragon?'

"What easy questions these are, to be sure! The dwarf says at once: 'The magic sword that the Father of the Gods made.'

"Now the stranger looks stern and says: 'But who shall mend the sword that it may be fit for the fight?'

"At this the dwarf is frightened indeed. He cries out in terror that he cannot do it, he knows no better smith than himself, and he does not see how it can be done. 'Then you should have asked me that,' says the stranger, 'instead of foolish questions about things that you knew already. Yet I will tell you: as none but the best of heroes could pull that sword out of the tree where it once stuck, so now none but a hero who knows no fear can put its broken pieces together. Your poor head, which belongs to me, I will leave to the same hero, and so good-by.'

"The dwarf falls upon the ground in a trembling heap, and so the young man finds him when he comes back to ask if he has yet mended the sword. 'I can never mend it,' he cries. 'Have you ever known fear?'

"'Fear?' he answers; 'no, what is fear? Is it something I ought to know how to do, something you ought to have taught me and have not? Is it a pleasant thing to have or to know or to do? What is it like?'

"'I cannot teach you fear,' says the dwarf, 'but I know one who can, or else you never can learn it. It is the dragon that lives in the cave at the end of the wood. I will take you to him and if he will not teach you fear then you may kill him.'

"'Very well,' says the young man, 'I will go; but first mend the sword for me; I shall need it.'

"'I cannot mend it for you.' the dwarf answers; 'only one who does not know how to fear can do that.'

"'Then I must do it myself,' says the young man, and he sets about it at once.

"The fire on that forge has never been so hot and the fire here on our hearth has never been so bright as now when the young man who knows no fear blows the bellows. While the coals under that eager blast shine redder and redder and then whiter and whiter he begins filing the pieces of the sword to powder. The dwarf cries out to him that that is not the way to mend a sword; but this is not a common sword, and the dwarf has shown well enough already that he knows nothing about mending it. So the young smith pays no attention to him, but goes on with his work. In mending magic swords, just as in some other things, knowing how at the start does not count for so much as not knowing any fear.

"So without any fear the young man melts the filings of the sword with the splendid fire which you can surely see just as well as anybody, and pours the melted metal into a mould of the shape of a sword blade. By this time the dwarf has found that it is of no use to interrupt him and has begun to think about his own work. When the dragon has been killed, he thinks, the hero will be hot and tired, and then he will offer him something to drink. It will be poison, the hero will die, and then he, the poor dwarf, who has worked and waited all these years for this day, will have all the treasure, with the magic helmet and the ring. So he sets himself to brewing the poison by the very same fire that the young man is using to forge his sword.

"And now the young man has heated the sword again and shaped it with hammers and cooled it with water, he is sharpening and polishing the blade and fitting it to the hilt, and now at last he holds it in his hand and it is done. He has forged the magic sword and has proved his right; he is the true hero, the hero who knows no fear. And is there any thing that such a hero loves better than a good sword? Yes, to be sure; but to this hero the time for that has not come yet, and he has never felt such delight as fills him now when he looks along the bright, smooth, keen edge of this blade. Oh, the sword was not like this before it was broken. Sometimes people say that beautiful polished things are like mirrors, but this sword is like a flame. It burns and twinkles as he holds it and turns it in his hand. I can scarcely see of what shape it is, for now it shines like a straight beam of light, now, as he twists it, there is a flash in a half circle, like a scymitar, and again the point alone gleams out and flashes, as if it would find its own way to the heart of a foe, with no hand to guide it. He swings the sword above his head, as he did the other that the dwarf made for him, and strikes it upon the anvil. And this time the anvil falls in two as if it were made of paper, and the sword glitters and shines and shimmers in the joy of its magic sharpness and strength.

"Now that the sword is ready, the dwarf leads the young man away through the woods, a long journey, to a place where he has never been before, to find the dragon. You see that deep, dark hole under the sticks; that is the dragon's cave in the side of the mountain. Just a little light shines at the very bottom of it, where the dragon is resting and breathing out fire. 'There is his hole,' says the dwarf; 'just wait here till he comes out and then kill him, Look out for his teeth or he will catch you and eat you; be careful about his breath, for it is fiery and poisonous; beware of his tail, for he may wind it around you and crush you.'

"'I do not care for his teeth or his breath or his tail,' says the young man; 'I only want to find his heart. Leave me here, and never let me see you again.'

"The dwarf goes away and the young man sits down on the grass to wait for the dragon. You see, since he knows nothing at all about fear it does not seem to him such a great thing to kill a dragon. He does not care much whether he kills it or not, and he is in no hurry about it. So he sits on the grass and looks at the gray old rocks and the bright young flowers about him, sees the golden sunlight falling in little spots and flecks through the branches, feels the cool, fresh morning air, and hears the soft rustle of the trees and the singing of the birds. Most of all, he listens to the birds that flutter about in the branches above him, as the sparks hover over the fire there, before they fly away up the chimney, and in particular to one bird, right over his head in the tree. It sings so loudly and so clearly that it seems to be talking to him, only, of course, he cannot understand what it says. He has wished for a long time that he might have some better company than the ugly dwarf, and he thinks now that he should like to talk with the bird.

"If he cannot understand the bird, perhaps the next best thing would be to make the bird understand him, so he makes a pipe out of a reed and tries to play upon it something like the bird's song. I don't know what he thinks he is saying to the bird with his reed, and he seems not much pleased with it himself, for he throws it away and blows a ringing, echoing blast on his horn instead. And now he gets an answer, for this time he has awakened the dragon, and it comes out of its cave to see what is making so much noise so early in the morning.

"Oh, but it is an ugly-looking monster! It is something like a snake, but more like a giant lizard. It has scales all over its body and it has a long, shiny tail. It walks clumsily, because its legs are too small for it, and writhes and wriggles itself along, raising its head now and then to look about, and breathing out red fire and black smoke like a blast from a furnace. When its poisonous breath has blown this smoke away for an instant, it shows two rows of teeth like knives and a long forked tongue like a snake's, and its jaws are opened wide enough to take the young man into them and bite him into a dozen pieces at one snap. Surely if he is ever to learn what fear is now is his chance.

"He sees all this just as plainly as I see it here in the fire; but do you think he is afraid? Why, he simply laughs at the monster. 'A pleasant-looking fellow you are,' he says; 'can you teach me what fear is? If you cannot, I shall prick you with my sword to make you think about it.'

"Now, this dragon can talk just as well as it could when it was a giant, so it begins to get angry and tells the impudent young man to come on and see what he can do with his little tailor's needle of a sword. He does not have to be asked twice, and in a minute there is just as lively a fight as you ever saw. The dragon tries to breathe fire upon the hero and scorch him up to a black cinder, but he does not want to be a cinder and he runs around to the dragon's side. Then the dragon tries to catch him with its long slimy tail, so that it may crush him to a jelly, but he does not want to be a jelly either, so as soon as the tail comes near enough he gives it a terrible wound with his sword, and then runs back in front of the dragon. The monster gives a dreadful roar as it feels the wound, and raises its head and breast high up in the air, striking at the hero with its long, sharp claws and trying to throw the whole weight of its body upon him. This is just what he has been watching for, and as the dragon lifts itself before him he drives his sword clear through its heart.

"Then he springs lightly away again, as the dragon, with another horrible bellow, falls down and rolls over upon its side. 'It is the curse of the ring that has killed me,' says the dragon, as it dies; 'my treasure is there in the cave; you can take it now, bold boy, but the curse of the ring will bring death to you, as it has brought it to me.'

"So the dragon lies dead. The young hero seizes the hilt of the sword to draw it from the dragon's body, and as he pulls it out the blood from the wound spurts upon his hand. It burns as if it were the fuel of the creature's fiery breath. As he feels its heat he puts his fingers into his mouth, and the instant that he tastes the blood the most wonderful thing of all happens to him. He understands the songs of the birds. The one that he tried to talk with before sings to him again, and now he knows every word. It tells him that in the cave are gold and jewels untold, that with the magic helmet he can do wonderful things, and that with the magic ring he can rule the world. He thanks the bird for telling him such good things, and goes to find the helmet and the ring. In a minute he comes back with them; he does not want the rest of the treasure, for he knows nothing about gold and cares nothing about it.

"Now the bird sings to him again. 'Beware of the dwarf,' it says, 'he means to do you harm. But when he speaks to you the blood of the dragon which you have tasted will help you to understand the meaning that is in his heart instead of the words that he says.'

"So the dwarf comes back, with a drinking-horn in which he has poured the poison, and he offers it to the hero to drink. But with all the friendly words that he tries to speak, he can hide nothing from the young man, who reads his heart and knows that he has kept him and fed him all these years only that he might kill the dragon, and that now he means to poison him and get the gold for himself. There is only one thing to be done with such wickedness as this. He raises his sword and with one blow strikes the dwarf dead.

"You can guess how the bird is delighted at this. It sings to him again: 'I know where you could find the loveliest woman in the world. There is fire burning all around her, and if you could only pass through that you could win her for your wife.'

"'But could I pass through the fire?' he asks.

"'Only the hero who knows no fear can do that,' sings the bird.

"'Very well, then, I know no fear,' he answers; 'the dragon could not teach it to me; lead me to this woman; perhaps I may learn it from her.'

"The bird flutters down a little from the tree and then flies away. Did you see the big, bright spark that flew up the chimney?

"Away runs the hero too, following the bird. It is a long journey, through the forest and over the rocks and the mountains, but he is young and eager, and his light heart makes the way almost as easy for him as it is for the bird. Yet the bird is the faster, and by and by it flies so far ahead that he cannot see it at all, and then his way is barred by a mighty form that stands before him. It is the Father of the Gods. The young man does not know what a terrible person he has met, though it is fair to say that if he did know he would not care, and he asks him if he knows where he may find the beautiful woman with the fire all about her.

"The Father of the Gods asks him in turn how he heard of this woman, what taught him to understand the song of the bird, who forged the sword with which he killed the dragon. All these things he answers, and the Father of the Gods is sure that the hero who knows no fear has come at last. Yet one test remains for him. 'There is the place you seek,' he says, as he points to the mountain-top, where the bright flames are whirling and dancing and leaping up into the very sky, 'there is your way, yet not another step upon it shall you go.' and he stretches his spear across the path to keep the young man back.

"Ah, once before that spear was raised against this magic sword. It was a mighty arm that swung the sword then, the arm of the best of heroes living, but the hero had done a wrong, he had helped to break a promise, and he who breaks promises can never break the spears of the gods. His arm had not the young strength of that which masters the sword to-day. Fierce and brave and noble was he, yet he had seen many sorrows, and he knew what fear was; the glad, free hope of the new hero was not his. The sword then was true of temper, bright and sharp, but the heat and the light of the fire of a new manhood had not been forged into it then, and it was not aflame with the glory of youth and the promise of love. And so, with a sweep and a flash as of lightning, the magic sword cuts through the spear that no other sword ever dared even strike, and as the fragments fall upon the ground, the mountain shakes and shudders, and the thunder rolls and rumbles about its top. The young man is again upon his way. Half sadly and half gladly, the Father of the Gods looks after him. He has come and has passed, the hero who knows no fear; he has not even feared the spear that ruled the world, and now that spear is broken. The time of the gods is near.

"Again I see the whole fire streaming up fiercely and joyously, as it did when the Father of the Gods kissed his daughter to sleep. The winds are still hushed around the mountain top, the flowers in the grass and on the rock still droop with folded petals, and the horse still sleeps upon the ground, for there, in the midst of the fire, on the bank of moss still lies the Daughter of the God, her form covered with her shield, and her face hidden by her closed helmet. Through all these years nothing has changed or stirred in this magic circle except the changing, stirring, restless, watchful fire that rings it around. Now, the time for life has come again. Up from the mountain side comes a ringing horn note, and in a moment the hero strides through the flames that dart and flicker and lick at him, but cannot harm him, and stands in the magic circle gazing in wonder upon its strange sleep.

"'Who is that,' he thinks, 'covered with the shield? It must be a knight, but is it not hard for him to lie there all dressed in armor?' He gently takes off the helmet and starts back in surprise as he sees the lovely face and the soft spun gold that falls out upon the moss as he lifts the helmet away. Now he raises the shield and tries to open the armor in front, that the knight may breathe more freely. He cannot unfasten it, and at last he cuts it with his sword, and then he starts again as he sees the light, snowy folds of the garment underneath. This can be no knight, this is a woman. What has he done? What shall he do? He stands and looks at her; he has never seen anything half so beautiful, and as he looks he trembles; he fears to wake her and he fears to leave her asleep. Yes, the hero who knew no fear trembles. He has learned to fear from this woman. Not by anything that she has done has she taught him, for she still sleeps. It is only because she is a woman that he fears. He is no less a hero for that. A man who lived long and never feared at all would be no hero. The time has come to him, as it must come to every man, when it is braver to fear.

"Yet, though he fears, he does not hesitate. He does just the only thing that he possibly could do. He kneels beside her and kisses her lips. Then she awakes. She opens those eyes that are blue with the depth of the sea and the light of the sky. She gazes around her at the rocks, at the trees, at the sunlight, at her hero, and her face is filled with joy. And what a face it is! No longer as it was before. At her father's kiss the goddess slept; her hero's kiss awoke the woman. Her face is as clear, as pure, and as radiant as before, but soft and gracious and gentle; her eyes are as full of light as they were, but there is tenderness in them too; her lips are as calm and beautiful, but they are all sweetness; what was still and stern and placid is full of sympathy, kind, and loving.

"The flowers lift up their heads and open to look at her; the horse neighs to say that he is awake again and knows her; the little winds come back and murmur softly at first among the leaves; then they get bolder and kiss her cheek and lift her hair and shake it out to the light, and whisper to her hero and ask him if he saw any gold like that in the dragon's cave. He has never seen any woman before, yet he knows that in all the world there cannot be another such as this. She has seen many heroes, yet this is he for whom she has waited so long. Each knows all the depth of the other's thoughts, and so they stand and gaze each into the other's eyes and into the other's heart."

"And is that all?" said the child. "It ends just like 'The

Sleeping Beauty,' doesn't it?"

"No; just here it is like 'The Sleeping Beauty,' but we shall see more some other time. This is the end for the night."

THE END OF THE RING

The fire has always fascinated and charmed me. When I was a child myself I used to watch it till my eyes ached, and my habit of throwing sticks and paper into it to see them burn was a terror to all my aunts. A bonfire was a delicious joy, and fireworks, especially if I could set them off myself, were the summit of happiness. Even now, whenever I see a house on fire I am afraid my pleasure in watching it is much greater than my sorrow for the people who are losing their property or their home. I do not want houses to burn, but if they must burn I want to see them. As for the fire on the hearth, that is my counsellor and friend. When we are alone together I sit and gaze into it, and it tells me of old, happy times, of other friends who are far away now, and of the pleasant nights we had together. It speaks to me of old hopes, it is glad with me in their fulfilment or it cheers me in their loss. It talks of bright, new hopes, and tells me that even if all else fails, it will still be true to me and will try, if I will come back to it, to cheer and help me again as it cheers and helps me now.

As I sat in this way with the fire, the little girl came and took a low stool beside me. She looked into the fire too, laying her cheek upon my hand, which rested on the arm of the chair. She does not care for our talks about other hearth fires that long ago went out, so we had to do something else to entertain her. "Did you want to know more about the Daughter of the God and the Hero who knew no fear?" I said. "Well, I can see them both now, just where we saw them last on the mountain top, with the fire burning around them as it did before, but not so high and fierce as before, because it is not needed for a guard so much as it was.

"The Daughter of the God is telling her hero that he ought to go to seek more adventures. Perhaps he may find other things for his magic sword to kill besides dragons and wicked dwarfs, and the more such things he does the better she will love him when he comes back. Oh, she knows all about heroes and what they ought to do. He does not like to leave her at all, but if he knows that she really wants him to seek adventures, you may be sure he will seek them. Before he goes, he gives her the ring that he got from the dragon's cave, with the curse upon it, but they are not the sort of man and woman to trouble themselves about curses. In return she gives him her horse and her shield, not that he will need it much against his enemies, with that magic sword, and besides she knows how to cast a spell upon him so that he cannot be wounded in battle; but the shield may keep off the rain, if he has to sleep out of doors. So he goes away down the mountain and she waits for him to come back.

"Now all the fire changes to a shining river. It is the same river where the treasure was once kept by the nymphs, only now we are above it instead of under it. On the bank is the hall of a king and I see the king himself sitting on his throne, with his sister, a beautiful princess, beside him. With them too is their half-brother. He is a strange fellow and you ought to know him. His father is the dwarf who stole the treasure, and his father has told him all about it many times and has taught him to hope that some time he may get it again, so that they two may divide all the riches between them, and with the ring and the helmet may rule the world. He is just as wicked as his father, all he cares for in the world is to get that treasure, and you may be sure that he will try to get it in every way that he can find, good or bad.

"He is trying at this very moment, and in rather a strange way, you may think at first. He is telling the king that he ought to have a wife, and that his sister ought to have a husband. The king asks, just as everybody always asks when he is told that, 'Whom do you want me to have?'

"'The most beautiful and the most royal of all women,' says the half-brother, 'lives upon a rock with fire all around it for a guard, and whoever shall break through the fire and come to her shall win her for his wife.'

"This does not encourage the king at all. He never walked through a fire or did anything of the sort, and he does not even care to try. You see the difference between a king and a hero. But the half-brother says that he knows of a hero who would be glad to go through the fire and get this woman for the king, if only he might have the king's sister for himself. The princess is not displeased at all at the notion of a husband who is so brave and can do such wonderful things, but she fears that such a hero must long ago have seen and loved some woman more beautiful than she, and that he will not care for her at all. But the half-brother answers: 'There is a magic drink which you shall give him, and it will make him forget any other woman he has ever seen, no matter who she is.'

"The half-brother knows very well, I believe, that the hero already loves the Daughter of the God, and it is she that he means to make him forget before he sends him to get her for the king. Of course the king and his sister know nothing about this, or they would have nothing to do with such a wicked plan, for they are reasonably good people. The half-brother says that the hero is going about the world to find adventures and is sure to come here before long, and true enough, even while he is speaking they see him coming with his horse in a little boat on the river. They call to him to come on shore, and they welcome him as if they were never so glad to see anybody before in their lives.

"Perhaps, indeed, they never were so glad to see anybody, and I am sure the princess never was. A form so full of life and action and vigor, or a face so full of freedom and courage and cheer surely she has never seen. The fine frankness of his ways and the young grace of his motion are new to her too, and that she can hope to win him at once for herself is almost more than she can believe. She would not think of such a thing at all if she knew how little he thought or cared about her. He is charming and polite enough, of course, but as often as he thinks of her or of anything else once he thinks of the Daughter of the God twice, and when his thoughts are not especially drawn away he thinks of her all the time. But now the princess offers him a horn filled with the magic drink that is to make him forget. Oh, if only that clever little bird were here now to warn him, as it did when the dwarf mixed the drink for him, how much trouble might be saved! But, you know, he never thinks of danger, so he drinks, and then he thinks of nothing at all - nothing at all but the princess.

"Well, that is not surprising, for you know she is only

the second woman he ever saw and he has forgotten the first. You would scarcely believe how much he has forgotten her. Why, if the king were to tell him at this moment that a woman slept under a shield, guarded by fire, that a young man came through the fire, cut open her armor, kissed her, awakened her, and vowed that he would love her forever, he would not remember that he had ever known of anything of the kind or had ever heard of such a young man. For him there is no woman in the world now but the princess.

"The king does tell him a little of this story, when the hero asks him, still thinking of the princess, whether he has a wife as well a sister. 'No,' the king answers, 'I have no wife. The woman I want for my wife I fear I never can win; she is far away upon a mountain and a fire burns all around her. He who could pass through the fire and come to her might win her, but I could never do it.'

"It is just as I told you. This absurd young man does not know that he ever heard of a woman in the middle of a fire before; he does not know that he ever learned to fear, so he says: 'I am not afraid of a little fire; I will go and get your bride for you if you will give me your sister for mine.'

"'I will give you my sister gladly,' says the king; 'but how is my bride to be made to think that it is I who come to her and win her, instead of you?'

"'That is easy,' says the half-brother; 'with that helmet which he wears he can take any form he will, and he can make himself look exactly like you. He shall bring the woman away through the fire and then he shall leave her to you, and she will never know that it was not you who came to her rock.'

"Now, the hero, you know, never knew what could be done with that helmet. He only took it with him from the dragon's cave because the little bird told him it was good for something. Now that he has learned its use everything that he and the king want to do seems simple enough, and they set off in the little boat for the rock with the fire around it. The half-brother stays on the shore and looks after them, with his pale face and his wicked eyes. The woman far away on that rock has the magic ring. When the king brings her here as his bride he will find some way to get the ring, and then what will he care for kings or brides, for princesses or heroes? He and the wicked dwarf, his father, will rule the world.

"The fire burns up high and clear again and within its circle sits the Daughter of the God. She does not sleep now; she sits and gazes at the ring her hero gave her, thinking nothing of the curse upon it, and wonders when he will come back to her. Ah, when will her hero come back to her? Do you remember how once on this very rock the daughters of the god met to ride together to his castle, and how they came each riding on her flying horse, racing with the driving wind and the hurrying clouds? With just such a leap and a flash of a sudden flame up into the smoke I can see one of them riding now. So quickly she gallops through the sky that I can scarcely see what she is till she reaches the rock, springs from her horse, and stands before her sister. Her sister runs to meet her and to ask if their father is still angry with her.

"The war goddess has sad things to tell of their father. He sits in his castle with the gods and his heroes around him. They do not go out to fight and kill each other, and to be made alive and well again at sunset any more. The Father of the Gods only sits there and looks at his broken spear, and the rest, full of dread, look only at him. He is weary of ruling the world, weary of all the trouble that has come from the wrong that he did in not giving that treasure back to the river nymphs. He is not sorry that his spear is broken and he would gladly hasten the end of all. He has made his heroes cut down the great ash tree from which his spear was made, the tree that spread its branches over all his castle, and they have piled the wood high around the walls. When the end comes it will help the castle to burn. And now the Father of the Gods says that, if the woman who has the magic ring whose curse has been so heavy would but give it back to the river nymphs, all his great sorrows would be over.

"This his daughter, the war goddess, heard, and hastened here to tell it to his daughter, the woman. Will she give up the ring? Will she help the gods to find the rest that they long for? Ah, but a war goddess knows as little of women as she does of men. No, no, the woman loves the man who gave her the ring and she would not lose it for a moment to gain ages of peace for the gods whose homes she shares no more. She cares nothing for weary gods; she has a hero. The war goddess cannot understand her sister. She leaves her and is away again, toward the castle of the gods, riding on her flying horse, galloping against the driving wind and the hurrying clouds.

"A horn sounds down in the valley. There is only one horn in the world like that, and the woman springs joyfully up to meet her hero. He comes and walks through the fire as he did before, but oh! how different he is from what he was before! Then his face was young and fresh and noble and his form was graceful and light; now his face and his form are those of the king. Is this the promise that the Father of the Gods made to his daughter? He said that none should ever come to her or win her but the bravest of heroes. Yes, this is indeed the promise and this the hero, but how sadly for her the promise is kept! When he saw her before he gently lifted off her helmet and kissed her and learned to fear before her; now he thinks only of the princess, away there by the river, and he tells the Daughter of the God that he is the king and that she must come with him and be his bride.

"She resists him, and he seizes her to force her. She holds out her hand to him with the ring and bids him beware its power, which will protect her from him; he seizes her hand and pulls the ring from her finger. She is helpless; she faints in his grasp; he carries her through the fire and down the mountain to where the real king is. He leaves them together and goes back alone to the hall by the river and to the princess.

"Very glad is the princess, you may be sure, to see him come back so quickly and so safely, and glad too is the half-brother, but for a different reason, for he sees the ring on his finger. Now they call all the people together to greet the king and his bride as they come in their boat on the river. There are shouts and cheers, and men with waving banners and women who scatter flowers; the king smiles upon his people and thanks them for their greeting, and there is only one who is not merry and glad. And whom do you think the king's new bride sees in all this happy crowd? Only her hero, in his own form again, and, if her heart was wounded and sad before, it dies within her now, when she sees him leading the princess out to meet them and knows that he thinks no longer of her. She turns pale and faint at first and then angry and fierce. She cries out that this man was her lover, that he has betrayed her for the princess and that he has betrayed the king too.

"Of course, nobody can understand that at all - nobody but the half-brother - but you can think how everybody must be shocked and astonished, and how everybody tries to make out what she means, and fails. To be sure, she understands it herself as little as the rest. She knows nothing about the magic drink that made her lover forget her; she knows only that he swore always to love her and that now he loves the princess. The king does not know that the hero ever saw his bride till he went to her mountain to bring her for him, so he supposes that, if he ever told her that he loved her, it must have been then; that would be betraying the king, his friend, in a most cruel way, of course. The princess knows only just what the king knows, and if the king has been deceived and betrayed, she must have been deceived and betrayed a great deal more. As for the poor hero himself, he does not remember that he ever saw this woman before, he does not know how he can have done any wrong, and he is more puzzled than any of the rest. Only the half-brother knows all about it, that nobody is to blame at all except himself, and it is he whom nobody thinks of suspecting. The hero lays his hand on the half-brother's spear and swears that he has never wronged anyone here; if he has, he says, may this very spear slay him.

"Now is the time for the half-brother to work the hero's ruin and to try to get the ring that he wears. When all have gone but him and the king and his bride, he whispers to her that he will help her, and will kill the hero to revenge the wrong that he has done her. 'You kill him!' she cries. 'If he once looked at you, you would not dare come near him.'

"'Yet,' he says, 'there must be some way that I could do it; tell me what it is and you will be revenged.'

"'I cast a spell upon him,' she says, 'so that he could not be wounded in battle, but I knew that he would never turn his back upon an enemy, so I set no spell there; you may strike him in the back.'

"Now, he tells the king that nothing but the hero's death can restore the honor that he has lost. 'To-morrow,' he says, 'we will go hunting; I will kill him with my spear, and we will tell the princess that it was a wild boar that did it.'

"'It shall be so,' they all cry; 'he must die.'

"And whom do you think I see now? The river nymphs again. Not before the king's house, where we have been so long, but in another part of the river, all shut in by wild woods and rocks. They are swimming and playing on the water, just as they did under it when we saw them first, and they seem just as careless and happy as they did then, but they are still mourning for their lost treasure and longing to get it back again. If they could only get the ring it would do as well as the whole treasure, for the ring is the magic part of it. And now to this very spot comes the hero, who wears the ring on his finger. He has wandered away from the king and his men, who were hunting with him, and as soon as the nymphs see him they beg him to give them back their ring.

"He says that he will not, at first; it was too much trouble for him to win it from the dragon. But he really does not care so very much about it, and I think he would let them have it in the end if it were not for a great mistake that they make in asking for it. They tell him about the curse of the ring, and that if he keeps it he will be killed this very day. Now, you can see easily enough that that is the very worst thing they could say if they hoped to get the ring from him, for he is not in the least afraid of being killed, and he will not have anybody believe that he is afraid. They shall not have it, he says, happen what will. They will have it, they call back to him, and this very day; and so they dive down under the water and leave him.

"Now come the rest of the huntsmen and sit about in a circle to rest here in the shade and to talk. The king is gloomy, thinking still of the wrongs that have been done him. His half-brother asks the hero if it is true that he knows what the birds say. 'I listen to them no more,' he answers; 'but to cheer the king I will tell you some stories of the things that I have seen and the things that I have done.'

"He tells them of the dwarf who kept him and brought him up that he might fight the dragon; he tells how he mended the magic sword, how he killed the dragon with it, and took the helmet and the ring from the cave. A bird then sang to him, he says, and told him that the dwarf would try to kill him, but he killed the dwarf instead. Here he stops, for he cannot remember anything about the mountain top with the fire around it, or the Daughter of the God, or even what the bird sang to him next. But the king's half-brother squeezes something into his wine and tells him to drink it and it will make him remember better.

"He drinks, and it does make him remember better. He tells of the lovely woman who slept with the fire all around her, and how he kissed her and awoke her. Then suddenly the king understands it all; he remembers the drink of forgetfulness that they gave the hero, and he knows that nobody has done any wrong but his wicked half-brother; he it was who told him of the woman in the fire who should be his wife, he who said that the hero should bring her to him, he who bade them give him the drink to make him forget, he who first said that the hero must die. The king would gladly save the hero now, but it is too late.

"It is too late, for of a sudden two ravens fly up from beside the river and away over the heads of them all. They are the ravens that fly all over the world and then to the Father of the Gods, to tell him all that they see and all that they hear. They are going now to tell him that the end of the gods, the end that he longs for, is near. The hero starts up to hear what they say. He turns his back to the others, and the half-brother, before the king can stop him, thrusts his spear into his back. The hero turns for an instant to rush against the murderer, but his strength is gone, and he falls helpless upon the ground. All the rest cry out in horror, and the half-brother turns from them and strides away.

"And what now of the hero? He speaks no word to those who stand about him as he lies here dying on the ground. Where are his thoughts now? He is thinking of the only time he ever feared. He is back again upon the rock, with the flames curling and whirling all around him. Before him once more lies the Daughter of the God. Again he kisses her lips. She awakes. He sees again those deep, blue, wonderful eyes. He does not see the rocks, or the trees, or the sunlight - only her.

Again for one last moment he knows that in all the world there cannot be another woman such as this. They look each into the other's eyes and into the other's heart. He is dead.

"They lay him on his shield and lift it upon their shoulders, and so they bear him back to the king's house by the river. The half-brother is there before them and tells the princess that her lover has been killed by a wild boar. She does not believe him, and when the others come she calls the king and all the rest his murderers. The king indeed wished his death once, but he is sorry enough for it now, and says that it was his half-brother alone who did it. 'Well, then,' cries the murderer, 'it was I, and now I will have my reward; I will take the ring.'

"The king cries out that he shall not have it, and draws his sword. The half-brother draws his own and rushes upon him, and before the men can run between them the king too lies dead upon the ground. Then again the murderer turns toward the body of the hero to take the ring, but, as he comes near it, the hand that wears the ring rises of itself, as if it were not dead and would ward him off. He falls back in terror, and so do all the rest.

"But now comes the Daughter of the God. She bids them all stand back from her hero. 'He was mine, not yours,' she says to the princess; 'he loved me and I loved him before you ever saw him.'

"'Then it was all the fault of this wicked man who has murdered him,' the princess answers; 'he gave me the drink for him that made him forget you.'

"She turns away from the hero and bends over the king, her brother. The Daughter of the God understands now; he was never faithless to her of himself. She tells the men to build a funeral pyre. They pile up the wood and the women scatter flowers upon it. Then she takes the ring from her hero's hand. While they lay his body on the pyre she bids them bring his horse, the horse that once was hers, that flew with her through the clouds when she was a goddess, and slept on the mountain top with the fire around it where she slept. With a torch she lights the pyre. See how the flames leap up and catch at the wood and stream and grow. Once more the ravens fly up from the river bank and away into the sky. Now the end for the gods comes indeed.

"The Daughter of the God springs upon the horse and with one bound they leap into the middle of the flames. Yet, as soon as they are there, they are gone, nor can I see the hero there any more. The pyre all falls together; but in the middle of its hot, red embers I see something brighter than all the rest. It is the ring. The water of the river rises and rises till it flows over the fire and puts it out. Then on the surface, swimming and playing about as always, I see the river nymphs. They have found the ring, and their treasure is their own again. But the wicked half-brother of the king, the son of that dwarf who stole it at first long ago, tries one last time to gain it. He plunges into the river to seize it from the nymphs, but one of them holds it up high in her hand and swims away from him, and the others twine their arms around him and draw him down and down under the water and he is seen no more. The river sinks back to its old bed. The treasure that was stolen is restored. All the evil and the punishment that came from the curse of the ring is done."

A big stick that had been burning brightly and steadily for a long time suddenly fell in two and the quick flames and the sparks sprang high up into the chimney. "See, it is the castle of the gods itself that is burning and lighting up all the sky. The wrong that they have done and the sorrow that they have suffered are past, and their end has come. But the fire burns fiercer still. It seizes upon everything, in the sky and on the earth. Perhaps it is better that it should. The world that we have seen in our fire here grew so selfish and cruel and bad after the gold was stolen from the river that it may be best for it to end in these flames. They will last for only a moment. Even now they are not so fierce. I can see the sky again. There is a beautiful brightness in it, like the coming of the morning; yet it is more than that, for it streams and flashes like the northern lights. I can see the earth again too, but it is not as it was before. It is a new world. It has all the beautiful things that the old one had, the green pastures and plains, the silver rivers, the blue mountains. Some of the gods have come back, but not those who did such wrong and made the old world so wicked. The God of Summer, who died long ago when the evil began, has come again; and if he and all who were good and beautiful before are to be here still, I am sure that the Daughter of the God and the hero who knew no fear must find their way here somehow. A new world that is to be all unselfish and brave and true needs such a woman and such a hero."

THE KNIGHT OF THE SWAN

The little girl was lying on the rug before the fire, one elbow buried in the long fur, and one cheek resting on her hand. She was gazing into the fire, studying the bright, flickering flames and the red embers. I had not noticed that she was there till her mother said, "You will ruin that child's eyes with your stories about the things in the fire. She would watch it half the day if I would let her; it is too bright and too hot to look at so long and so near. Come away, dear, and don't look at the fire again to-day."

"But why can't I see such things as you see?" the child said to me, with a little sigh, as she got up slowly from the rug and came toward me.

"Just because you have not quite learned how yet," I said; "now suppose you give up trying for a little while, because you might hurt your eyes, as your mother says, and let me look into the fire for you again. Sit here in the big chair with me; turn your face right away from the fire and lay it against my shoulder. Now shut your eyes. Some people can see a great deal better with their eyes shut, especially such things as we are trying to see, because when their eyes are open they see the every-day things all around them, and it confuses them and prevents their seeing what they want to see or what they ought to see. They are people who have not learned to look right through the everyday things and see others, in spite of them, that are much better and more beautiful, as you will learn to do some time. But just now keep your eyes shut.

"I see then, first, a splendid company of knights and people. The shining of the fire is like the light of the sun, that glances from the polished armor, the gleaming weapons, the standards, and the banners of bright-colored silk and gold. It is all so fine that it looks like a holiday time; but it is not that, for the crowds of people seem bent on something more important than dancing and playing games. They are all looking toward the King, who stands under a great tree and seems to have something to say to them. The heralds are blowing their trumpets and calling to the people to come and hear what the King has to say, though they are all there already and are only too anxious to hear, and so the King speaks. He says that far away at the other end of the country there is danger. Enemies are coming against him and his people, and he calls upon all the men here about him to help him to guard the and.

"Then they all shout and wave their banners and their arms, as I can see in the flickering of the bright little flames, and they all cry that they will fight for their King and their country. But this does not satisfy the King, for he says that since he has come here he finds everything going wrong and everybody quarrelling, and he asks what it all means. Now there comes forward a man who has all this while been standing silent beside his wife; and it may be as well to say just here that this man's wife is a wicked witch and that the man himself is none too good. So a part of what he tells the King is true and another good large part is not true at all. When he tells what the King knew before, he tells the truth; and when he tells anything that the King did not know before, it is generally a lie.

"So he tells the King that he was left the guardian of the two children of the Duke who ruled in this part of the country, and who died a few years ago. One of the children was a girl and the other was a boy, and he tells the King, too, how he took care of them as they grew up. All this is true and the King knew all about it before. But now he goes on to say that one day, when the brother and the sister had gone away from their castle together, the sister came back alone, trembling and crying and saying that she had lost her brother. Probably this is true enough too, but when he says that the poor sister was not really sorry at all, because she had killed her brother herself, he is telling a dreadful, cruel lie. Still perhaps it is not so much his fault, for his wife, the witch, who you must remember is a good deal more wicked than himself, knows much more about it all than it would do for her to tell, and she may have deceived him as well as other people.

"Of course the King is shocked at such a dreadful story as this, and he wants to know how the sister could ever have done anything so wicked. Well, of course the man who accuses her so boldly has a reason to give for what he says she did, or he never would have dared mention it at all. So he explains that the sister was to be married to him and that she refused him, and then he married the witch instead, only he does not call her a witch. He thinks that the sister must have had some other lover, and she must have thought that if her brother, who ought to be Duke as soon as he should be old enough, were only dead, she could be married to her lover, and then he would be the Duke. And now he says that he thinks he himself ought to be Duke, since there is nobody who deserves to be one better than he, and he asks the King to make him so. Now, of course anybody as bright as you are can see at once that the whole reason for all these wicked stories is just that he wants to be Duke; but kings and knights and crowds of people are not always very bright, though they may look so there in the fire, and they do not feel so sure about it as you or I would. So the quarrel lies between a rich and powerful man who is a soldier and once saved the King's life, with a wife who is a witch and knows all about magic, and one poor girl who knows nothing about magic and who has no friends who would dare to help her. For these people here about the King are a peculiar sort of people who shout very loud about justice and their own rights and others' rights, but seldom do anything unless they feel sure that they are on the side that is going to win. There are no such people nowadays, of course; but there were once.

"But the King himself is a good king, and he means to be quite fair and just, and he calls for the sister to come before him and tell her own story. So the heralds blow their trumpets again and call for her, and she comes. She is dressed all in white, and she looks so beautiful and pale and sad that nobody who was not wicked himself could ever suspect her of doing anything wicked, and all the men about mutter that the one who says that she killed her brother will have to prove it. They have just heard the King say something of the kind, so they feel very righteous and very bold about it. The King, then, asks her if she can say anything about this dreadful accusation, and she tells him how often she has prayed for help, how, after she has prayed, she has fallen into a sweet sleep and has seen a knight in bright armor, leaning on his sword, and how he has comforted her. This knight, she says, shall be the one to fight for her and to protect her.

"Now, of course, this is all very pretty, but it does not seem to have much to do with the question of whether she killed her poor little brother or not. Yet it does have something to do with it, and I will tell you how. A long time ago, hundreds of years, when people had quarrels, they did not hire lawyers to argue and plead and plot and contrive for them, but they just stood up together, if they were both strong men, and fought till one of them killed the other or showed that he could if he wanted to. And everybody who looked on felt perfectly sure that the one who was right could not possibly lose such a fight and the one who was wrong could not possibly win it. If one of the two who had the quarrel was a woman, some friend who trusted her enough to think that she was right would fight for her."

"But what made the man who was wrong ever fight at all," the little girl asked, "if everybody believed that he was sure to get beaten?"

"I have thought of that myself," I admitted, "and I think that it must have been for one of two reasons: either the bad people did not believe that the right was sure to win, or else the people who were wrong usually thought that they were really right. I believe that was the true reason, and it shows that bad people are not always quite so bad as we think, for they usually contrive in some way, I am sure, to make themselves believe they are right. And now, though all these things that I am telling you are things that I see right here in the fire, yet they are like things that must have happened long, long ago, and this very way of settling disagreements by a good hard fight is the way that the question of this poor girl's guilt or innocence must be settled. She probably knows this just as well as anybody, and that is what she means when she says that the knight she saw in her dream shall be the one to fight for her. But the accuser turns everything against her, as usual, and says: 'You see it is just as I said; she is talking about this lover of hers who she hopes will marry her and be Duke instead of her brother. Yet he says he is quite ready to fight anybody who wants to try it with him, and he invites any of the men standing about to come forward and fight for the poor, helpless girl, if he wants to. But they all say no, they should be very sorry to have to kill such a great man and so brave a soldier. The truth is, you see, they are all afraid that if they should fight they might get hurt, and why should they trouble themselves about this girl's rights or wrongs?

"Still she says that the knight whom she saw in her dream shall be her champion, and if he will come now and help her in this need she will be his bride if he will take her, and he shall have all her father's lands and his crown, since her brother is dead. But nobody comes, and the people all begin to think that she must be guilty after all, and that, instead of the accuser having to prove that she is, she will have to prove that she is not, if she wants any sympathy from them, though why she should want it I hardly know. But the King still means to give her every chance, and he orders the heralds to blow their trumpets toward the north and the east and the south and the west, and to call upon anybody who will defend her straightway to appear. And the heralds blow their loud trumpets and the people gaze anxiously in all directions, but nobody comes to help her. And then she tells the King that her knight dwells far off and does not hear, and she begs him to call upon him again, and the heralds blow once more, and she prays that her knight may be sent to her, and now suddenly all the eyes of the crowd are turned one way, and all the people shout and point and gaze at something which they see away in the distance.

"I can see it too, for there in the fire, back on the hearth, is a bed of bright embers that shines and glitters like a broad river under the sun of noon, and at the very farthest place is one little spot brighter than all the rest, and it seems to come nearer and nearer, and as it comes I begin to make out its wonderful shape. There is a little boat, and in it stands a knight, all in silver armor, and it is his armor that shines so. But the strangest thing of all is that a beautiful white swan, its wings almost as bright as the knight's armor, is drawing the boat along by a silver chain wound about its neck. It is this that makes the people gaze and point, and, while the swan and the boat are coming nearer, I will tell you more about the knight than he will be willing to tell about himself. Did you ever hear of the Holy Grail? It was the crystal cup, the old stories say, out of which the Saviour drank at the Last Supper, and afterward His blood was caught in it, as He hung upon the cross. Hundreds of years later it was kept in a beautiful temple which nobody ever knew how to find, except a few chosen knights, who guarded the Grail and did its bidding, for this cup seemed still to have the life of that blood in it, and it had ways of telling its knights what they must do. And so they were sometimes sent far away to fight for the right or to punish wrong, but wherever they went they never knew hunger or thirst or weariness, and they could never be killed or overcome in battle; but no one must ever ask one of these knights his name or his dwelling place, and, if anyone having the right should ask these questions, the knight must return to the temple of the Holy Grail. Now, seven days ago a bell in the temple rang, all of itself, meaning that help was needed somewhere. One of the knights put on his armor and called for his horse, and stood ready, but he knew not where he was to go or what he was to do, till a swan drawing a little boat came sailing along upon the river, and the knight said: 'Take back the horse; I will go with the swan,' and so here is he come to see what help is wanted of him.

"And now I see him step on shore, and the girl whom he has come to rescue knows him as the knight of her dream, and everybody is glad of his coming except the accuser and his wife, the witch, and she, strangely enough, seems a good deal more frightened at the sight of the swan than at that of the knight. Now the knight asks the young girl whether, if he will fight her battle and win it, she will promise never to ask him whence he comes or what he is, and she swears that she will always love him and trust him, and will do whatever he commands. So now the two knights, with all the people looking on and holding their breaths with anxiety, and the king watching that all may be done fairly and in order, draw their swords and stand against each other. But I see only one or two little flashes of the flames as the gleaming swords are whirled above their heads, and then the wicked accuser falls and the Knight of the Swan spares his life, while all the people shout and lift the knight above their heads on his shield, just as if they had known all along that the girl was innocent, and just as if they would not have shouted just as loud if the battle had gone the other way.

"The fire is going down a little and everything looks darker. It is night now. Here on one side is a church, all dark, and on the other side, where the light still shines, I can see the bright windows of the palace, where they are making preparations for a grand wedding tomorrow, and you can guess who are to be married. On the steps of the church, looking up at the palace windows and the lights that shine in them, are the witch and her husband. He is bemoaning his disgrace and accusing his wife of causing it all by telling him that the good sister had killed her brother. And this shows me, more than anything he has done before, how bad he is, and what a coward he is, because, when a man has tried to gain things that he knows are not his by ways that he knows are not right, he ought to take all the consequences, if he fails, like a man, and not snivel and say that a woman made him do it. But the witch says that there is a chance yet for them to be revenged, for, if only the Knight of the Swan can be made to tell who he is, he will have to go away as he came and be lost, and she believes she can find some way to tempt his bride to ask him the forbidden questions, and then he will have to answer.

"Now the bride that is to be to-morrow comes out upon a balcony of the palace, and the witch, sending her husband away, calls to her and tells her how sorry they both are for all that they have done. No doubt they are very sorry indeed, as they ought to be. But the bride is so happy and so kind that she cannot bear to see anybody unhappy, so she says that she forgives them, and if she has injured them in any way she asks that they forgive her. That is absurd, of course. Then she lets the witch talk to her till the wicked woman says that she hopes the knight who came to her in such a strange way, that nobody can account for, will never deceive her, and that she will always live happily with him; and by this she means, of course, that she thinks that he will deceive her and that she will not be happy. But the bride says that she trusts her knight wholly, and she asks the witch to come in with her and rest for the night. And that is just the one thing she ought not to do, for here is what I hope you will see and remember more than anything else in all this: be as kind and as helpful and as compassionate as you can, always, but never help, never listen to, never allow to be near you a man or a woman who says one word against anyone you love. Put no trust in anyone till you know that trust is safe, and, when you once know, never hear of one breath of doubt again.

"The fire burns higher and brighter, and the morning is coming. The square grows light and fills with people. Now come the heralds again, and they sound their trumpets and proclaim that the Knight of the Swan is to have the crown of his bride's father, and is to be called Guardian instead of Duke, that the accuser of his bride is an outcast and must be shunned by all men, and finally that everybody to-day is to come to the marriage, but that to-morrow all the men must go to the defence of the King and the country. And now, with all its sparkle and glitter, comes the procession, leading the bride to the church, when, just as she is at the door, right before her stands the witch, full of anger and pride, and cries aloud that it is her place to go before this woman, and no one shall keep her from the place that is hers, and she taunts the bride with not knowing who or what her knight is; and so a great clamor arises among the people, and in the midst of it come the King and the Knight of the Swan and their train. The witch's wicked husband comes, too, and calls out that the knight beat him yesterday by magic and not by honest fighting, and he demands that the King ask the knight who he is. But he and his wife are put aside, and the procession goes into the church, and as I look into the church itself now the whole of the fire is a blaze of candles on the altar. Now turn your face away from the fire as it was before and shut your eyes again. There is no more to be seen in this wedding than there was in the battle of the two knights, and all that there is I will tell you.

"The light of the candles on the altar changes to a blaze of wedding torches, and the King and the knights and the ladies are leading the bride and the bridegroom to their chamber. Slowly and solemnly, yet joyfully, they march along, and it is all so clear to me that I can even hear the music that they chant as they come. Soft and low it is at first, and then it swells out fuller and stronger and clearer but always so noble and pure and stately in its melody and its rhythm that nobody who had once heard it could ever forget how grand and beautiful it was. I have heard it many times, and you will hear it often, too, and once, I hope - I almost know - you will hear it at one of the sweetest moments of your life, and whenever you hear it I think it will be more full of meaning for you if you will think of the Knight of the Swan and his bride. But do not think of what comes to them afterward, for that need never come to you or to anyone who remembers what I told you a little while ago; and if ever you feel tempted to forget for one moment, then think of this true and lovely music - you will know it well and can think of it when you like by that time - and I am sure you will feel truer and better again at once.

"But the torches pass away and out of sight, and the knight and his bride are left alone; and now comes the sad part, for the poor bride has listened too much to those who spoke evil of her husband, or something evil has come into her own mind and made her forget her promise, for she tells him that she loves him so much that she wishes she might know what he is whom she loves. Now this may be very natural and might be very right if she had not promised never to ask; but though he begs her not to demand of him this one thing, yet she implores him more and more to tell her, till at last she speaks very cruelly to him, and as much as tells him that he does not love her at all. You would never think that she was the same poor girl who knelt by the river and prayed that her knight might be sent to help her in her danger. And suddenly, as he is about to tell her all she asks, her old accuser breaks into the room with his men, and rushes with his sword drawn to kill the knight, and now indeed his bride does seize his sword and hold it out to him, while he draws it from the sheath; then there is one little flash of a flame as he swings it high above his head, and his enemy lies at last dead before him. He tells the men to take him away and to lead his bride before the King, where he will come and tell her everything.

"It is morning again on the banks of the river, and the knights and the people are coming in crowds as I saw them in the beginning. The King comes, and the poor bride, sadder now even than she was at first. The Knight of the Swan comes too, and he asks the King if he did right to kill his wicked enemy, who was trying to kill him unprepared. The King answers that he did right. Then he says that he cannot go with the King to his wars, because his bride has forgotten her promise to him, and has asked him whence he came, and now, by the law which he obeys, as soon as he has answered her, he must leave her and all the rest forever. Then, while they all listen in sorrow, he tells them that he is a Knight of the Holy Grail, and must go back to the temple which he left to come here and help his bride. And while she weeps at the thought of losing him, suddenly I see the swan again on the river, drawing the little boat as before, ready to take the knight away, and then he tells his bride that if she could but have trusted him and never questioned him for a year, her brother would have come back to her.

"And now for one last time the witch stands up, more proud and revengeful then ever, and cries out that she has beaten them all, for the swan is really the brother, and that it was she who wound the chain about his neck that enchanted him and made him a swan. But while she exults in her triumph, there flies down over the heads of all of them a beautiful white dove. It is the dove that comes once a year to the temple and strengthens the power of the Holy Grail, and as the knight sees it he kneels and prays and then rises and unwinds the silver chain from the swan's neck, and at the very instant the swan is changed into a beautiful boy, the lost brother, and he runs to his sister and they clasp each other in their arms, while the witch falls down upon the ground, overcome at last and powerless, and the knight steps into the boat, the dove lifts the silver chain, and they glide away upon the river, farther and farther, and the little spot where they were, that was the brightest in the fire, grows dimmer and fainter and goes out and is dark."

"And won't the knight come back at all?" asked the little girl.

"No," I answered, "the brother and the sister are close in each other's arms and they are gazing away upon the river as far as they can see, but the Knight of the Swan will never come back."

THE PRIZE OF A SONG

The fire was almost out. It was so late in the spring that none at all was needed, but we liked it to look at. As for the little girl and me, we should hardly have known how to get on without it, and the little girl's mother chose to humor us, so we wasted a great deal of wood, as ignorant people would think, and were just as comfortable with the sky smiling and the trees budding all around us as if we had been in the midst of snow-drifts and howling storms. This afternoon the sun had been shining right in upon the fire, as if he would like to know what it was doing there at all, when he was making the weather quite warm enough, in the house as well as out. A fire never burns well when the sun shines on it, and besides, nobody had taken much care of ours, so that after the sun had gone it looked very low and discouraged.

"Do you think anybody could see anything in a fire like that?" the little girl asked, with a doubtful gaze into it and a meaning, clearly enough, that, if I thought it at all possible for anybody to see anything, she wished that I myself would try.

"We will put on another stick," I said, "and have a better fire. It will not be a very hot fire even then, and with all this soft spring air about us, I don't think we can see any more gods and giants and knights and dragons in it. But we may see some simpler people, with bright young hearts that begin to stir and move and to beat quicker and harder in the spring, as young hearts ought to do, not only in the spring of the year, but in their own spring, and we may perhaps see some people with older hearts, which stirred and beat too in their time, and we shall see by them that those which move freest and grow warmest in their spring are the fullest and the richest in their autumn and can never be hurt in the winter, just as the tree in which the sap flows best in the spring spreads out the broadest shade in the fierce heat of the summer, bears the finest fruit in the autumn, and lives the strongest till the next spring comes. If you ever tell any very learned people what we see here in this fire they may tell you, perhaps, that it all happened on Midsummer Day and not in the spring at all, and they will be quite right, in their own poor way of being right, but Midsummer Day is not in the middle of the summer, you know, but just at the beginning of it, when the spring has been gone only a few days. It is then that the lovely touch of the spring has done all that it can for the world, when the sun climbs his very highest in the heavens to look at all the sweetness and beauty that have been spread over the earth, when the summer is young and happy and kind and has not begun to burn and wither everything that would like to love its brightness and its power. So if you would see all the joy and the light that the spring can bring, you must look for them not far from Midsummer Day.

"We shall not begin to see all this till our new stick begins to burn better, but in the meantime we may see some things that are pleasant enough, if they are not quite so radiant, and while the fire is still rather dark, just burning quietly in a few little places, we seem to me to be in a dim, old church. The service is just ending. In one of the pews sits a pretty girl who is behaving herself in a most unbecoming way, for she is constantly sending shy glances toward a young man who leans against a pillar not far off and looks at her in his turn in a way that really ought to shock her, instead of pleasing her, as it seems to do."

"Is he a knight?" asked the little girl, instinctively knowing him for the hero of the story.

"Do you want him to be a knight?"

"Oh, yes; let's have just one knight, if we can't have any giants or dragons."

"I believe you are beginning to see the pictures in the fire yourself. Well, he shall be a knight, but he shall not wear any armor and he shall not fight, and all the rest of the people we see shall be quite common people, mere tradesmen, a goldsmith and a tailor and a toy-maker and a cobbler and the like. But whether the young man is a knight or not, he and the pretty girl ought to know better than to look at each other in that way in church, with looks that seem to mean so much and yet to have no connection with the service at all. The service is over now and the people all leave the church, except a few, but the young knight and the pretty girl stay behind, and he does not lose a minute in telling her that he loves her and that he is dreadfully anxious to know if she can love him. Now, of course, as she has done nothing all through the service but steal glances at him and probably could not even tell what hymns were sung, or whether there was a sermon or not, and has been thinking all the time how handsome he was, and knows very well that he was looking at her all the time, and knows very well, too, being a pretty girl, that he was thinking how pretty she was, of course, you see, she could not tell at all whether she could love him or not, and such a question naturally throws her into the greatest confusion.

"But while the young man is saying all the pretty things that the time allows, and the young woman is trying to think what she shall answer, her maid, who has been running about all this time, looking for things she has lost, bustles up, hears a part of what the young man says, and tells him that her mistress is already betrothed; and the mistress quickly says yes, but that nobody yet knows to whom. This is such a surprising state of things that it needs an explanation; so the maid tells the young knight that her mistress is to be given as bride for a prize to-morrow, which will be Midsummer Day, to the man who shall sing the best song. He asks if the bride herself is to judge whose song is best; and at that she makes up her mind at last, and says that she will choose nobody but him. But there is something else, for nobody can even try for the prize unless he belongs to a certain company or society of poets and singers here in the town, and the knight, though he has a pretty good opinion of the song he could make if he should try, is quite a stranger here. And now, as if for the very purpose of helping the knight, comes another young man, who turns out to be a prentice, and he begins arranging benches and chairs in some queer sort of way, while the looks that he casts at the maid and the looks she throws back at him show that they are not total strangers; and he tells them that these very poets and singers are to meet here in a few minutes, and that if anybody wants to join them he will have a chance to sing to them and to prove whether he is worthy.

"So the young man of course determines that he will try, and it is clear that he expects nothing in the world but that he will carry everything before him; and while the young women hurry away, the prentice tells him something about the singers, who are always called masters, and the queer rules that they have for making all their songs. Queer enough they are, too, and so many that if you were to hear them all you would think that they were quite enough to prevent anybody's ever making a song at all; but the most important thing that the knight learns is that, while he is singing, the judge will make a mark with chalk every time he breaks a rule, and, if more than seven chalk marks are scored against him, he cannot be a master, and so cannot try for the prize that he wants so much to win to-morrow.

"Now the masters begin to gather for their meeting, coming in one by one and two by two. First comes a goldsmith, the father of the pretty girl we have just seen. With him is a queer-looking, awkward, self-conceited man, who, anybody can see in a minute, must be a town clerk. From what he is saying to the goldsmith it is clear that he means to try for the prize of his daughter's hand to-morrow. He is in no doubt that he can sing better than anybody else, but is not sure that the goldsmith's daughter will think so. That is a very unlucky thing that happens to singers sometimes; they themselves know perfectly well that they can sing better than anybody else anywhere about, but all the other people are so stupid that they will not understand it.

"The young knight, who knows the goldsmith, tells him now that he wants to join this company of singers, and be a master too; and the goldsmith says that he shall be glad to help all he can. But the town clerk overhears them, and he sees at once that what the knight wants is to sing for the prize to-morrow. Now, the rule is, you remember, that nobody but a master may even try for the prize; so the jealous town clerk resolves that he will keep the young man from becoming a master. And it happens, by good luck for him and bad luck for the knight, that it is his turn to-day to take the chalk and mark the mistakes that are made in singing by anybody who tries to prove himself worthy to be a master.

"When the masters are all met, the goldsmith makes a little speech, and tells them how the prize is to be given to-morrow. They are to decide who wins, but his daughter is to judge too. She may choose none without their voice, but she may refuse any. That is no more than fair, of course. No girl would like to be married to a man just because the lines of his poetry came out right when somebody else counted them. Yet the masters all argue and dispute and suggest about the rules; but in the end they agree to do just what the goldsmith says, since they cannot do anything else.

"Now comes the trial of the young knight who wants to be a master. The town clerk goes behind a curtain, with his slate and his chalk, and you may be sure he does not forget his promise to himself that the knight shall fail. Then the young man stands up in the midst of them all and sings his song. A happy, free, beautiful song it is. It tells first how the spring came into the forest and awakened the trees and brought the flowers. Then it tells how the spring came into the young man's own heart, as you know I told you it ought to do, and how it made him sing of love; and that is quite right too, though perhaps I forgot to say so before.

"But happy and beautiful as the song is, it is scarcely begun before the most dreadful scratching of the chalk is heard behind the curtain. All the masters begin to shake their heads, too, for this knight is bold enough to make his own song in his own way, and he knows and cares no more about the rules and measures of these masters for making songs than you know or care about the game laws of Scotland. So by the time the song is half over, out rushes the town clerk with his slate, not with the eight marks on it that would end the singer's hopes of being a master, but with nearer eighty. He vows the case is hopeless, and as he shows the slate to the other masters they all seem to agree with him, though they are not all quite so jealous as he is.

"All but one; for there is one old shoemaker who says that he thinks the song was very good. It did not follow the rules, but it had rules of its own, and he liked it. Then there is trouble indeed. For any man to say in this old church and this old town that a song can be good when it has one line too many or one rhyme too few is almost as bad as for him to say that the King is bald-headed and that the oldest princess has freckles. All the masters say that to let such a song pass is out of the question, and that the shoemaker is quite absurd to think of such a thing. At this the shoemaker declares that the town clerk is not a fair judge, because he is jealous. At that again the town clerk says that the shoemaker had better not talk so much about poetry, but go home and finish the shoes he has ordered. Now, the shoemaker is really the only one of all the masters who knows anything at all about poetry; but now and then, years ago, a man who knew a great deal had to stand aside and let others, who knew very little but could talk louder, do what they liked in their own way. That is what the shoemaker has to do now, and for this time the knight has failed.

"What a bad fire we have, to be sure! It is getting lower and lower, and even our new stick will not burn. While everything is as dark as this we shall have to think that it is night. Never mind, we can see a little still, and the little that I can see is the street of the old town, with its queer old houses and peaked roofs and sharp steeples. Here, on one side, where there is a bit of light shining like a glow in a window, is the shop of our old cobbler; and over there, with no light at all, the fire is so bad, is the goldsmith's house. The cobbler is sitting outside his door, trying to work; but the light is as bad for him as it is for us, and, besides, he cannot think of his work, much less do it. He is thinking, I know, of the young knight and his song, and is wishing that he might win the prize to-morrow, master or no master. His heart had its spring-time once, you may be sure, and its glowing summer, and they have brought it a rich, peaceful autumn, such as they alone can bring. That was why he knew all the meaning of the song and liked it, though it broke every one of his own rules. And so, like the good old fellow that he is, he wishes the man who sang the song all joy and good luck - and the prize.

"While he is thinking of all this, comes the goldsmith's daughter, for she has heard that the young man has failed, and she is sad, and wants to talk to some one. Perhaps, too, she wants to know something. They talk about to-morrow, of course, and the shoemaker tells her that the town clerk means to sing for the prize. At that the prize herself gets quite alarmed, for she likes the town clerk no better than you or I do. 'But why should he not win?' the shoemaker says; 'there will not be many bachelors there to try.'

"'And might not a widower try?' she asks slyly.

"Now, the shoemaker knows that she means himself, but he says no, he is too old. And then the absurd girl actually urges him to try, though she does not want him the least bit, and does not want anybody except the young knight, who makes such beautiful songs that are all out of shape. When you get to be a woman, perhaps you will know why she does this; but I confess I do not. Perhaps she thinks that the shoemaker would not be half so bad as the town clerk, or perhaps she only wants to find out if the shoemaker really does mean to sing, so that she may know whether he is the knight's friend or his enemy. At any rate, he pretends to be not half so much the friend of the young people as I know he really is, and when she is beginning to get quite angry with him her maid comes and tries to lead her into the house. But just at this moment the knight himself is seen coming down the street, and not a step toward the house does she go after that.

"The shoemaker has gone into his shop now, and the lovers are alone. He tells her how he sang his very best, that he might be a master, because that was the only way to win her, and it was of no use. But she does not care whether he failed or not. She declares that he is a poet, that she will give the prize herself and to nobody but him; so now what do you suppose it matters to him if all the masters in the world said that his songs were wrong? He will not sing for them, and they need not listen.

"There is just one way now, as anybody can see, for him to make sure of the prize, and that is to take it while he has it. And that is just what he is about to do. But I am sorry to see that the cobbler, behind the door of his shop, has been impolite enough to listen to all this important talk about poets and songs; and he sees that if he lets these two run away together now, there will be no prize and no singing for to-morrow. So he sets a lamp in his window, right there where the fire is kind enough to burn for us a little at last, and sends the light streaming out across the street, and the lovers know that if they try to pass they will be seen. And while they are helping each other think what they can do, somebody else comes slowly down the street, walking in the shadows and looking around to see if he is watched, like a burglar. It is the town clerk, and he has come here just to sing under the window of the goldsmith's daughter the song that he means to sing to-morrow, to see if she will like it and if she will probably give it the prize. Oh, he is a good, honest poet and faithful lover, and he means to leave nothing untried that can help him. One does not get a chance to marry a goldsmith's daughter every day.

"All this is annoying enough, but there is nothing for the lovers to do but to wait for the town clerk to sing and go away; so they get into the deepest shadow, and then they put their arms around each other so that they can stand closer and not be seen so easily. It is a good plan for another reason, too, because some people can wait much more patiently in that position than in any other. But things are getting worse and worse, for the shoe-maker seems bound to have his part of the fun too; and just as the town clerk is about to sing he begins to work again and to hammer on his last. This is the most impolite shoemaker, I suppose, that this polite old town ever saw, if he is a poet. Think of a man who will hammer on a shoe when a town clerk is going to sing, and a song that he made himself, too. Something must be done, of course; so the town clerk comes and talks with the cobbler, and pretends that he is very anxious to get his opinion of the song he is going to sing. That seems natural enough, because everybody knows that the cobbler is the best poet in town. So they agree that whenever the town clerk breaks a rule in his song the cobbler shall strike one blow on his last, just as if he were marking the mistakes on the slate, the way the town clerk himself did with the knight.

"Oh, but he must be a good town clerk, he knows so many tricks, and can always arrange everything so well to make it go his way. The town is lucky to have such a clerk. Yet, strange to say, the minute he begins to sing, he makes more mistakes than even the poor young knight did, and it is really a question whether his song or the shoemaker's pounding makes the more noise. Mind, I say noise, not music; if it were a question of music the shoemaker would be far ahead. Well, between them, they wake up the shoemaker's prentice, and he comes to the window of the shop, to see what is the matter. He is the same prentice whom we saw in the church, who looked at the goldsmith's daughter's maid in such a strange way, you remember. And now, as he looks across at the house opposite, he sees the goldsmith's daughter's maid again, standing at the window. She is standing there in one of her mistress's gowns, to make the town clerk think that the mistress herself is listening to his song; and he does think so, but the poor prentice knows who she is very well indeed. And since he knows who she is, of course he makes up his mind at once that the town clerk is singing to her, that he loves her, and that just as likely as not she loves him. No doubt you think he might know better; and perhaps he might, if he were not so much in love with the goldsmith's daughter's maid; but when a man is in love he is always ready to believe anything that it is particularly uncomfortable for him to believe.

"So, what does the shoemaker's prentice do but jump right out of the window, fetch the good town clerk one blow under the chin, that shuts his mouth and stops his singing, and begin just as lively a fight with him as any we ever saw among our knights and giants and dragons. They make so much noise that more people wake up, and come out of their houses into the street; and, since the old town is usually a bit dull and quiet, they find this just the sort of thing they like, and they all begin fighting, too, with a jolly good will. Of course, not one of them has the slightest notion of what he is fighting about; but that makes no difference to any good, honest fighter, and there is a fine breaking of heads and kicking of shins. Just as everything is in the most delightful confusion possible, the knight and the goldsmith's daughter try to make their way through the crowd and escape; but the troublesome old shoemaker, who has been watching them from the very beginning, runs quickly out, pushes the girl to her own door, where her father stands to receive her, drags the knight into his shop, seizes his prentice too, and shuts his door behind him. Somebody cries that the watchman is coming; the people scatter right and left, and, by the time that little flame there under the andiron has burned up and shown itself to me as the old watchman's lantern, it shines on nothing but the quiet, empty street.

"But there is more light than the watchman's lantern, for our new stick is beginning to burn now. The night must be past, and, if the night is past, it is Midsummer Day. It is not so bright yet as it might be. Let us put on still another stick, and have all the Midsummer weather we can. I see a room now, not very handsome or rich, but very comfortable and cheerful, with flowers in the window and more flowers scattered about. It is the old shoemaker's shop, and the old shoemaker himself sits at the window, pretending to read, but really thinking, as usual, about the young knight who sings to please himself and not to obey other people's rules, and about the goldsmith's daughter; and he is trying, also as usual, to plan some way to make the prize go as he wants it to go. He does not quite see how it is to be done, but he has a comfortable feeling that it will all come out right; and while he is studying over it, the knight himself comes put of the room where he has slept to say good-morning.

"He tells the shoemaker that he has had a beautiful dream, and the shoemaker asks him what it was, saying that it is the true business of a poet to have dreams and to tell them, so that everybody may know them. So the knight tells his dream, making it into a song as he goes along, and now and then the shoemaker stops him quietly to tell him what are the rules of the masters for making such songs as this. The knight always asks why such rules should be, and the shoemaker gives him some pretty reason for each one, and he shows that the rules are not so bad after all, if only one knows how to use them and to make the most of them. The dream was about a beautiful garden with a tree that bore fruit of gold, and as the dreamer looked at it there came a lovely maiden, who you may be sure was the goldsmith's daughter, and she embraced him and then pointed to the fruit of the tree, and when she pointed to it, it was golden fruit no longer, but stars, and the tree itself was a laurel-tree.

"You may guess that the poor old masters never heard

such a song as this. As the knight sings it the shoemaker writes it down on a bit of paper and tells the knight to remember the melody, and then they go away together. Scarcely have they gone when the door opens softly and in a treacherous-looking sort of way that must be strange to the shoemaker's door, and in comes the town clerk. Ridiculous enough he looks in his gorgeous holiday clothes, and limping along, because of the beating that the prentice gave him last night. And angry enough he is, too, with the shoemaker and the prentice and the knight and the world in general, except himself, with whom it might be reasonable for him to be angry. You can see a wicked red glow, right there in the middle of the fire, where he stands. But he has not forgotten about the prize - oh, not in the least. He is still plotting and contriving how he can best make sure of it, and so it does not take long for his sharp little eyes to find the song lying on the table, where the shoemaker left it when he went out.

"Now, there is one peculiar thing about these people who can see through mill-stones, and that is, that they sometimes think they are seeing through one when there is really no mill-stone there at all; just as you and I might think we were looking through a glass window when it was only an empty sash. Just see, for instance, how much cleverer the town clerk is than there is any sort of need for him to be. He sees that this song is a song; well, anybody could see that. He sees that it is in the shoemaker's handwriting; anybody who knew the shoemaker's handwriting could see that. But now he takes the liberty of guessing that the shoemaker made this song himself, and that he is going to sing it himself for the prize. So he gets more angry still, for he knows that the shoemaker is the best poet in all this dear old town, where anybody can be a poet by learning the rules, and he knows that if the shoemaker tries to win the prize he will probably do so. But he hears the shoemaker coming back and he has just time to hide the song in his pocket.

"Now he boldly accuses the shoemaker of meaning to sing for the prize. It may seem to you that it is no affair of his whether the shoemaker means to sing or not, and it may seem so to me too, but we are not town clerks. Yet the shoemaker assures him that he does not mean to sing, accuses him in turn of stealing the song, and then, to prove his own words, gives it to him. With that the town clerk is altogether delighted, for he is one of those shallow people who think that when one man has done a good thing, another man can do just as well as he by doing the same thing. He feels sure that if he sings one of the shoemaker's songs he cannot fail to win the prize, and he makes the shoemaker promise that, whatever happens, he will not claim the song as his. The shoemaker is quite ready to promise anything, because he is a wise old soul and he knows that it is not altogether what one does, but pretty largely how one does it, as a cobbler or as a town clerk or as a singer, that wins him fame and honor - and Midsummer Day prizes.

"The town clerk hobbles away, and now who should come in but the goldsmith's daughter herself? Well, no one could wonder at her lover's having pleasant dreams, for she is as pretty a prize as ever a poet sang a song for, or to, or about. With her best gown and her flowers and her jewels, and especially with herself, I don't think you could find any prize that a poet would rather have, even in a town twice as big as this. It seems there is something wrong about the shoe that the cobbler has made for her to wear to-day, and she has come to get him to mend it. I wonder, by the way, if she knows that the knight was the shoemaker's guest last night. She says that when she wants to standstill the shoe insists on walking, and when she wants to walk the shoe makes up its mind to stand still. You see yourself what a remarkable and improper way this is for a shoe to behave. It is so strange that I am inclined to doubt if it is the fault of the shoe at all, or if she really knows whether she wants to walk or stand still. You see it is not easy for us to tell just how a girl would feel at being put up for a prize.

"While the cobbler is at work on the shoe, the knight too appears, and the cobbler hints that he should like to hear the rest of the dream that the young man began to tell him before. So he sings more of his song and tells how the stars among the branches of the laurel-tree formed a crown for the lovely maiden's head, how her eyes, as he looked into her face, were to him brighter than all of them, and how then she twined with her own hand, about his head, the wreath of the star-fruit of the laurel-tree, and still and always he saw her eyes brighter than the stars.

"After he has sung this they all seem to understand one another better. The goldsmith's daughter's maid comes in to look for her mistress, the prentice tumbles in to look for the maid, or for something else, and away they all start for the fields outside the town, where all who will - that is, if they are masters and may - are to sing for the prize.

"At last the fire is burning as it ought, and we can see all the life and light that we care to enjoy. Those flames that stream up so far must mean that the sun has mounted his very highest to mark the noon of

Midsummer Day, and the floods of merry sparks that pour up the chimney are not brighter or merrier than the throngs of people, men and women, boys and girls, that walk and run, and caper and dance, and tumble out of the city gates and into the meadows where the singing is to be. But there is more gravity all at once when the masters come. They are mighty and important persons at any time, and above all they are so to-day, when they are to decide who is to have this wonderful prize. They have a higher place to sit than the rest of the meadow, and the common people of the town, who do not pretend to be poets at all, can stand wherever they can find room. The goldsmith and his daughter have the highest seats of all, and the shoemaker is next to them, for he is supposed to know a good song when he hears it. All the other masters have good places too, including the town clerk. The knight is somewhere in the crowd of people who know nothing about poetry.

"When everything is ready the town clerk is the first to sing his song for the prize, because he is the oldest of those who are to try, and indeed he seems to be about the only one, with the knight quite out of the race, because he did so badly in the church yesterday. So the town clerk stands forth, and after a little opening plink-plunk on his guitar, he tries to sing the knight's own song, which the shoemaker gave him, knowing well that he would get into trouble with it. And indeed, the dream that he tells about must have been a nightmare, though nobody who hears him knows what it is about, and the poor town clerk seems to know least of all. He has the song under his coat and tries to look at it now and then, but he reads it wrong and sings nonsense, and in a moment all the people are laughing at him, even those who do not know a good song when they hear it, for they seem to know a bad song very well when they hear it.

"At that he gets angry, stops singing, and says that the song is not his at all but the shoemaker's, and he is to blame. Here is a fine state of things, for the shoemaker is supposed, as I said before, to know more about songs than any of the other people in town, and indeed he knows more about most things than all of them put together. He says that the song is not his, but that it is good enough, if only it could be sung right, and he asks if there is anybody here who knows how to sing it.

"This is the time for the young knight, and he comes forward from the crowd and says that he will try. But first, the shoemaker makes all the masters promise that if he sings the song well and if it is a good song he shall have all the honor just as if he were a master. Now the young man takes his place and everybody is still. He looks straight at the goldsmith's daughter; he does not know that there are any others around him; and now he sings. And what a glorious song it is, full of hope and happiness and victory and joy! He did not sing like this to the masters in the church yesterday; not even to the shoemaker this morning did he sing like this. It is not hard to see the reason. Yesterday he tried to be a master, and when he sang he was wondering how these fussy old fellows would measure his song with their rhyme-gauges and their foot-rules. How could anybody sing when he was thinking of that? Even then it was not a bad song and the goldsmith's daughter would have known it if she had been the judge. The shoemaker, with his warm old spring-time heart, knew it as it was, but the masters were too learned ever to know anything. But now the goldsmith's daughter is the judge and the young poet sings only to her, only for her, only about her. If one smile curves her pretty lips as he sings, it is more to him than the shouts of all the people. That is the way to sing, and that is why, when he is done, all the people do shout, and do clap their hands and wave their hats, and do cry out that he must have the prize.

"And he does have the prize. She crowns his head with a wreath of laurel, which he cares for only because she sets it there, and the goldsmith himself brings him the gold chain that makes him a master. This the young man would put aside, but the wise old shoemaker bids him take this too, and to honor the masters and their art; for, he says, though the Holy Roman Empire should vanish in smoke, yet art will remain. And I think he means by this that all the kingdoms of the earth may be lost and may fall into dust and ashes, as our fire here will do when we leave it to-night, but that the happy young people, with their stirring hearts of spring, and the kindly old people, with their ripe hearts of autumn, will still sing songs and still tell stories."

THE BLOOD-RED SAIL

The fire had been out for weeks. Somebody who came from the country had almost filled the fireplace with a huge bouquet of wild roses. They made it look very pretty for a few days, but now the roses had all faded and fallen to pieces too, and nobody cared enough even to sweep up the dry, dead leaves and throw them out. It all looked forsaken and desolate enough. But it was no more desolate than I. We were lonely and unhappy for the same reason, the poor fireplace and I, because the little girl had gone away with her mother down to the sea and would not be back for more weeks and weeks yet. The city was so hot and dull and stupid! It made me feel dull and stupid to stay in it, except when it made me angry. Yet perhaps the fireplace was even a little worse off than I, though it was not more forsaken and alone, for it had no work to do, while I had plenty. Then again the fireplace, in spite of all the wonderful and beautiful things we had seen in it sometimes, had never been anywhere except just where it was now, and it knew nothing about the sea. But I had been in several other places; and even in the city, with the heat pouring down from the sky and quivering up from the pavements, one can dream of "waters, winds, and rocks," and dreams are good things to have for those who can have nothing else.

And I had the dreams and something else. For the little

girl and her mother had said that I might come down to the sea too, whenever I thought the city could get on without me. What surprised me was that the city got on at all, but all the time I thought more and more that I was of no use to it, and it was of no use to me, and finally I left all my work in it to take care of itself and fled away to the sea. Oh, how lovely it was! That first long unbroken sight of the line where the sky and the water met made me feel, as I always feel at such times, that it was worth half the year's worry and care just to see this ocean and this heaven, to breathe this free, salt air, to smell the flowers by the roadside, and to gaze and gaze again at the two great tracts of peaceful blue. How wonderful is this calm rest of a thing that can rage and destroy when it will! The peace of a field of daisies is pretty and sweet; the peace of the ocean is like that of God.

The little girl and I had a long walk along the beaches, over the rocks, and through the tall, salt grass. We hunted among the smooth, round pebbles for the smoothest and the roundest; we studied the jelly-fish that was borne up the beach by the wave and then glided swiftly back again with it, as if it had forgotten something, till one wave, higher than the others, would leave it lying on the sand at our feet, where we could study it as much as we liked; we wondered if the jelly-fish ever did forget anything and if he had remembered it now, so that he did not want to go back any more. We caught little crabs and made them run races, laying huge wagers on our favorites; I filled my pocket, and the little girl filled her handkerchief with the tiny, pointed shells that can be strung into such pretty necklaces. Then we found a great, bright, curly ribbon of seaweed, as wide as two hands, so long that when the little girl held it by the middle she could scarcely lift the ends off the sand, and rich and beautiful in color like dark-red tortoise-shell. The little girl looped one end of it around her head and wound the rest about her body, so that she looked a true little sea princess.

All day a fresh, cool breeze came up from the sea, so different from the air of the dreadful city. Toward evening it grew cooler yet. The wind blew more, and little shreds and patches of fog, and then larger clouds of it, hurried along over the fields. We could see them coming, away off over the water, then they reached the shore and hid the walls and the pastures, then they wrapped us up within themselves and passed us, and we saw them flying off again as if they were trying to carry a chill from the sea as far into the land as they could. And it was chilly after the sun was quite gone - not very cold, but just cool enough so that everybody thought it would be pleasant to have a bit of fire on the hearth. And when we thought a fire would be pleasant we always had it.

Of course down there we never think of making a fire of anything but driftwood. It makes the most wonderful, magical fire in the world. One could dream out stories for a whole evening from the wood alone. Here is a stick that must have been a part of a spar. Was it blown away from the mast in a gale? Now hold your breath and think if some poor sailor was blown off into the waves with it. Did he catch at this very stick as he sank? Did his wife wait and wait for him at home, till his shipmate came and told her? Here is a little piece of smooth board, with a bit of cornice fastened to the end. It must be from the wall of a cabin. Did the captain's daughter and the young mate sit under it and whisper stories to each other in the calm evenings of the voyage? There is a piece of barrel-stave. Perhaps it once held rum for the sailors' grog; it burns as if it did. There again is a float from a fisherman's net. Was the net torn when it broke away, and did the fisherman lose some fish? And because of that did his sweetheart perhaps lose a ribbon or a trinket? Then here is a broken fragment of a lobster pot. Even this might be some loss to a poor man. And not only are all these things and a hundred times as many more to be thought of, but all this wood has been soaked in the salts of the sea, and when it burns the flames are of all sorts of strange and beautiful and ghostly colors - white and red and green and blue and yellow and violet.

Everybody feels the charm of a driftwood fire. The little girl surely could not help feeling it, and she came and sat on the stool at my feet, leaned her head against my knee, and gazed at the flames without saying a word. But I answered her thought. "Yes," I said, "we may see almost anything in that fire. Look at that strip of cocoanut husk. Does it not tell of green palm-groves and sunny skies and warm breezes? Yet as it lies there on its curved side, with the two ends lifted from the hearth, has it not the shape of a galley, like those in which the rude old pirates of the North used to sweep over the sea, bringing terror to all who came in their way? It is all burnt and blackened, and right over it rises a tall flame of bright red. It is a black ship, with sails all of the color of blood. The strangest of ships it is, and it has the strangest of stories.

"Long, long years ago, in a fearful storm, the captain tried to sail this ship around the cape. The captain of another ship hailed him and asked him if he did not mean to find a harbor for the night. But he swore a terrible oath that he would sail around the cape in spite of Davy Jones, if it took till doomsday. At this Davy Jones was angry, and swore on his part that it should take till doomsday, that the captain should sail in the storm till then and should never get around the cape. Do you know who Davy Jones is? He is the wicked spirit of the sea. When the winds and the waves rage and tear away the sails of the ships, or sink the ships or drive them upon the reefs, it is his work; when it is all smooth and calm and sparkling, as we saw it to-day, then the good fairies of the sea are there and are making everything about it calm and happy.

"But the fairies never came near this ship. She was always driven about, and there was a storm wherever she went. Never could her captain bring her into any port and never could he round the cape. Only for years and years he sailed and sailed in the storm, and found no harbor and no rest. At first he was bold and tried to sail on and gain his port; then he was angry and raged again, and swore that he would not be beaten; then he was in despair; and at last he grew so weary with the storm and the sea and the clouds and again the wind and the sky and the ocean and yet the rain and the waves and the fog, that he longed only to die and to be at peace.

"But he did not die, and no one of his crew died. The sailors all grew old, and their hair and their beards were white, and they looked like ghosts, and their ship was like the ghost of a ship; but they were not ghosts; they were real men and they sailed in a real ship. Sometimes the crews of other ships saw them. Sometimes they hailed the crews of the other ships and begged them to take letters to their friends at home. They said that their almanac had been blown away and they did not know how long they had been from home.

They would lower a boat and row to the ship they had hailed, in a sea that would swamp any other boat in half a minute, and so they would bring their letters on deck. Those who knew their story refused to take the letters, and then the sailors would nail them to the mast or lay them on the deck, with a heavy weight to keep them from blowing away, and go back to their own ship. So the letters sometimes reached their homes, for it was said to bring bad luck either to take their letters willingly or to throw them away when they were left on the ship.

"But oh, what of those to whom the letters were sent? Once a captain brought a packet of them to the port from which the strange ship had sailed. Not one of those to whom they were directed could be found, and he opened some of them, hoping that the letters themselves might tell him some way of finding the sailors' friends. One of the sailors had written to his father that after this voyage he meant to live on the land with him and never to go to sea again. When the captain took this letter to its address, he found a man of the right name, but the man said: 'No, no, the letter is not for me; no son of mine is a sailor. None of our family ever went to sea except one, for there is an old story that my great-grandfather's brother once went away in a ship and that the ship was never heard of again. For years his old father used to dream about him and to declare that his ship still floated, and he died believing that his boy was yet alive. No, that is my name on the letter, but it is not for me' One sailor had sent a bank-note to his sister, but where her house stood there was a church, and it had been there for a hundred years. Another in his letter sent a pressed tropical flower to his sweetheart. It was of the color that looked pretty in her hair, but the poor fellow forgot that pressing it would spoil it for that. The captain, despairing of delivering the letters, went into the church, and there, on one of the stones of the floor, he read the sweetheart's name. It said that she was ninety years old when she died, and the words were almost worn away by the feet that had crossed them. The captain dropped the flower upon the stone, and the next morning it was swept away.

"So the sailors grew so old that it seemed they could not grow any older. Then slowly they began to know what they had always refused to believe, that they had been sailing for years and for hundreds of years, and that all who ever knew them and loved them had been long, long dead. Then their eyes grew more hollow, and their hair and their long beards thinner, and their faces more wrinkled and withered, and it was as if all the blood had dried out of their hearts. Perhaps it was when the blood went out of their hearts that it stained the sails that dreadful red. So much for the crew, but it was diffcrent with the captain. Davy Jones was preparing something worse yet for him, or thought he was. He was tired of seeing him simply wander hopelessly on the ocean; he wanted to plague him more. He could do this, he thought, by giving him now and then a little hope and then shattering it and sinking it to the bottom of the sea, and dragging the man's heart to the bottom of the sea, too, with a leaden load of despair.

"The captain had never grown to look old, and now, to carry out his wicked plan, Davy Jones promised that once in every seven years he might enter a port and go on shore, and if ever he should find a good woman who would love him and give her life for him, he might rest and never sail again; but when he failed to find such a woman he must go on board his ship again and sail through the storm and the wind and the waves for seven years more. Now, Davy Jones would never have promised this if he had thought that there could be such a good and loving woman, but being only a wicked spirit of the sea he did not know much about good women.

"And for a long time his plan did succeed and the poor captain was more wretched than ever. Once in seven years he would go on shore to seek that true woman, and as often he would return to his ship and sail away. Good women he found many, but none of them would love him. Then his heart would fill with bitterness, for he saw them loving and giving their lives to men who, he could not but know, were less brave and patient and worthy of them than he; faithless men who forgot them, cruel men who misused them, dull men who knew not their own blessings. Why should they love such men as these and never him? Now, you and I, who are so wise, know, of course, that such thoughts were selfish and wicked. For what was he to any woman that she should give her life, or even an hour of it, for him? Was his life or his peace better than another's, that another's should be given for his? Why should any woman love him when there were so many others for her to love?

"But he never thought of these things, so he would rage against all women and he would steer his ship into the most awful waves and whirlpools, hoping that she would be wrecked and sunk, but his ship was never harmed; and he would steer toward pirates, hoping that they would kill him for the chests of gold he had, but even the pirates, when they saw his blood-red sails, would cross themselves and flee from him. Then the seven years would pass and he would go on shore, and now, perhaps, a woman would say that she loved him; yet when the time came she would not give her life for him, and he would throw himself down upon his face on the deck of his ship and steer nowhere, but still drive on through the wind, the black waves, the black storm, and his own blacker despair."

"Oh, my!" said the little girl, "that's awfully nice and ghosty, but I thought this was the best fire we ever had, and now you don't see anything in it at all."

"Oh, yes, I do," I replied, "I have seen the ship all the time, that black ship with its sail of red flame. I have seen it tossing upon the sea, sweeping up till the flame of its sail almost touched the clouds, and then plunging down into the black water, but always, always rushing on with the storm around it and with never any rest. And I have seen the angry clouds tearing across the sky; you can see them yourself when the smoke flies up the chimney, and then when the white flames are flickering and flashing up and then dying down, you can think that you see the lightning. Yes, and you cannot help hearing the wind, whistling up there around the top of the chimney as it would whistle through the rigging of a ship.

"The seven years have passed again, and now the ship has come to land, that the captain may try the little chance once more that has failed him so often. The red flame has dropped down, for the sails are furled, and the wind has stopped for a minute, too, while the ship is at anchor, and there is no need for the storm to pursue it. I see the captain walking on the shore and talking with the master of another ship that is anchored near by. The master tells him that he lives only a few miles away, and asks him if he will come and spend the night with him on shore. The captain replies that for a little rest at his house he will give the master untold treasures from his ship. He makes a sign to his men and they bring a big chest. He opens it and shows the master that it is full to the top of gold and pearls and rubies and emeralds, that flash and shine with all the colors that ever our driftwood fire can show us.

"Such a price for a night's or a year's lodging the master never dreamed of. He cannot believe that such wealth is all for him, and he asks what he can ever do for the captain to earn it. 'Have you not a daughter?' the captain asks. You see he knows how to go about his work without loss of time, even though he has never been very lucky in it.

"'Indeed I have,' the master answers, 'a good, true, lovely girl.'

"'Give her to me,' says the captain, 'for my wife; that is all I ask.'

"The master thinks that is a good deal to ask, but not too much, when he looks at the chest again, and he says, joyfully enough: 'You shall have her, indeed; I know such a man as you will make a good son-in-law; come home with me quickly.'

"So each goes on board his own ship. The master sails first to lead the way, and then the red flaming sail springs up again and the black ship is off the shore. And the storm howls again too; the waves rise, the clouds tear across the sky, and in a minute the ship has passed out of sight.

"Listen to the wind around the chimney. It was roaring and whistling a minute ago, but now it is not so loud. It grows fainter still, till its sound is no more a roar or a whistle, but only the lightest humming of a wind, and to me all the wind seems gone now and it is the hum of whirling spinning wheels that I hear. And what I see is a room where a dozen girls sit spinning and singing songs about their wheels and about their lovers. But one among them does not spin. She lets her wheel stand idle and only sits and looks at a picture that hangs on the wall. It is of a dark man with black hair, a black beard, and deep, piercing eyes; it is the captain whom we have seen so much already. The other girls laugh at her, say that she is in love with the picture, and ask her why she does not sing with them. She cannot sing their happy songs, she says. Then they ask her to sing by herself, and she sings them a song about the captain. It tells them his story, as we know it already, and as she sings they all stop their wheels and begin to gather around her, and in spite of all their merriment it moves them at last, as such a sad story ought to move anybody.

"And when she has finished they all say, 'Ah, poor fellow, if only some good woman would save him from his dreadful lot! But who would do it and give up her own life?'

"'I would do it,' she replies, 'and I hope that the winds may blow him here, so that I can tell him that I am ready to love him and to save him.'

"The others, who are very charming girls, no doubt, but just now not quite so noble and resolute as this one, are almost frightened to hear her talk so, and when somebody says that her father is coming they all slip away and leave her to meet him alone, while they chatter among themselves about what a strange girl she is to want to give her life for a man whose black hair and piercing eyes she has never even seen except in a picture. Her father is the shipmaster whom we saw, as you have guessed by this time, and he has brought the stranger captain home with him. 'This is my daughter,' he says; 'is she not all and more than all that I told you?'

"Then, having always found her, no doubt, a good and obedient child, he tells her at once that the captain is to stay with them, and that he expects her to be his wife. Some girls do not like to be ordered to marry even the men they love; but she is so true and simple and kind that she means to love the captain with all her heart, and even her father's wish that she shall do so cannot change her. The father thinks very wisely that they will get on better without him, so he leaves them, and they do get on better at once. First they gaze for a long time into each other's eyes, those deep, piercing, sad eyes of the captain, and those true, soft, young eyes of the master's daughter. Then he thinks that her face is not strange to him, as he remembers, dimly at first and then more clearly, that he has seen this face in dreams many times, when it was the face of an angel who was to save him from his long weariness. And the dreams were not far wrong, for she looks into his eyes with no thought for herself, but only: 'This is one who has suffered for many years and must suffer for many years more, unless I love him and save him.'

"He asks her if she can give herself wholly to him, and she answers that, whatever his fate may be and whatever hers, she will take it all and will be all his own forever. 'If you knew what it would cost you to be true to me,' he says, 'you would shrink away from me and try to save yourself.' 'Never,' she answers; 'let it cost what it will, I will be true to you till death.'

"I see the shore and the sea again. This time it is near the master's house, and the two ships are moored not far apart. The red sails are furled, but on the ship there is the little pale blue flame of a ghostly watch-fire. The captain comes out of the house and strides up and down along the shore. All the gladness that he had when we saw him last is gone - no, not all, but there is doubt and perplexity with it now. The fact is that the captain has learned something now that he never knew before. All these weary years he has been longing and hoping for some good woman to love him, but he has never thought much about loving any good woman. What right had he to expect anything when he meant to give nothing? He has never thought of this before, but he thinks of it now. And the reason is that now, when he has found a woman who loves him and will gladly die for him, he finds too that he loves her as well; and if he loves her, how can he let her die for him? She is so good and unselfish that perhaps it would be a happiness to her to do it, but it is the more to his credit that he does not think of that.

"That is why he paces up and down the shore and fights hard with himself. Only think of it. For all these many years, while other men were living happy lives and growing old, and their children and their grand-children were growing old too, the angry winds and waves have driven him about and have given him no rest; now this woman could save him, but his love tells him that he ought to save her instead. Can he save her and go back again to the rage of the storm and live in it forever, live in it till doomsday? Oh, it is a hard fight, but at last he answers yes; all that he has borne so long he can bear still longer. The sea shall swallow his ship and cast it up again, the clouds shall sink down upon it, the winds shall drive it over the whole ocean, but she shall not die because of him. And it will not be with him quite as it was before; now he will remember through all the hundreds of years that are to come that she loved him once, he will think of her always, and thinking of her he will wait for doomsday.

"I see him go on board his ship again; he is calling to his men; they are hoisting the sails; see the red flame spring up again. The storm comes again too. Look at the black smoke that is like flying clouds, and hear the wind up there around the chimney. But now out of her father's house comes the master's daughter. She sees the ship speeding away, and in an instant she knows all the reason; she knows it because she would have done the same if she had been the captain. Then she runs to a high rock that stands out into the sea; she calls through the loud wind that drowns her voice that she will come to him and will be true to him till death, and then she leaps from the rock into the rough, raging waves. But look; the waves that very instant are rough and raging no more; the sea is all still; the clouds are gone, and the wind is silent. The ship with the blood-red sails is sinking out of sight. See how the red flame dies down and the black hull is breaking to pieces. And right where it was I can see the captain and the master's daughter rising out of the sea together, with a beautiful light around them, as beautiful as all the colors of our fire can make it. They seem to float along the water, away and away, and I think the good fairies of the sea must be taking them to Fairyland or to some pleasant island, where they will always live happily together."

The fire blazed up brighter than ever for a minute and then dropped down again. "Come here to the window," I said; "see how the fog has all cleared away and has left the moon shining down upon the sea. What a broad track of light it makes from the shore here where it is nearest us, away off to the edge of the sky! How the little flecks and sparkles of light run and dance and chase one another, and how happy and glad they seem, riding the little ripples of waves in the light of the moon! Are they the sea fairies, dancing and playing together and calming the water, to bring the sailors safe back to their homes, do you think?"

THE LOVE POTION

There was a beautiful moon and everybody said it was a pity to have it wasted. So indeed it was, and everybody asked everybody else what we should do to prevent its being wasted. A few, who had made the best possible use of more moons than the rest of us, were in favor of simply sitting on the rocks and looking at the moon and the sea under it. That was really not a bad plan at all. When you sit with somebody beside you and the rest of the party not too near, on a high rock that runs far out into the water, and look at the big white moon and the soft colors of the sky around it, and then at the stretch of water, unobstructed to the horizon, with the moon's reflection broken by the waves into a million dancing sparkles, when you turn and look toward the beach, seeing the black surges rolling swiftly up to the shore and then breaking into gleaming foam, but still plunging on, like banks of tumbling snow - then indeed you can think of wonderful things and say wonderful things if you like. But perhaps you may prefer to say nothing at all, and that is a very good and pleasant way too, for at such a time it seems really not quite right to talk unless you can talk in poetry, and that is not easy to do, no matter how much you may feel like doing it.

These people who had made the best of so many moons knew all this, but some of the others thought that this moon was worthy of a greater effort and a more deep-laid plan. All the things that are usually done on moonlight nights were rejected one by one. Then one of those strange persons who are always noticing things said, not at all as if he thought it had anything to do with the subject, that there was an uncommon quantity of wood scattered along the shore. Then it was decided, just because nothing better could be thought of, that there should be a bonfire down on the shore, and nothing else, except the moon. So in the forenoon the daily bathing party started for the shore a little earlier than usual, and instead of spending our extra time in lying on our backs with the sun in our eyes, in the hope of getting sunburned, we spent it in gathering wood for the fire.

Picking up driftwood for a bonfire is not very easy work, but there were so many of us that we soon had two good piles, one for the fire at the start and one to feed it as it burned. Among the wood there were two whole barrels, and one of them had had tar in it, so we were sure of a splendid fire. Then we all went home, and after it was dark we all came back again. The fire was lighted; the bright-colored flames of the driftwood played together and grew and streamed up above our heads, crackled and roared and sent up torrents of black smoke mixed with golden sparks. For a little while nobody was tired of feeding it and watching it, but by and by we let a few attend to keeping it up, while the rest of us made a very little fire among the stones and let it quickly die down to a bed of red embers for toasting marshmallow drops. The man up at the village who keeps the shop with everything in it, and the post-office, must have a notion that city people live chiefly on marshmallow drops, that is, if he ever lets himself be troubled by any notions except those he keeps to sell.

After that the most of the people strolled away along the shore. Some said they wanted to see how the fire looked from a distance, and others, I think, were trying to get nearer to the moon. At last the little girl and I were left alone. We made cushions of folded coats and shawls, and sat leaning against a big rock, looking at the fire.

"We scarcely need the fire to-night," I said; "if we try a little we can see pictures through it and all around it, as well as in it. See that big, black rock, that stands almost in the edge of the water, like an old castle, built upon the shore. Then look away across the water to the island over yonder. I see a ship coming from the island toward our shore; perhaps you do not see it yet. As it gets nearer I can see a knight standing in the bow. He is a big, bold, fine-looking fellow, and he is all in black armor. The ship reaches the shore and the knight and his men go toward the castle, where the King lives, while the King and all his court come out to meet him. Some people may tell you, or you may some time find out for yourself, that this King is a very wicked man, mean, cruel, and treacherous. Perhaps he is, but all I can tell you is that now he does not seem so to me; on the contrary he seems as kind and generous as you could wish.

"The knight in the black armor marches proudly up to him and tells him that he has been sent by his brother, the King of the island over there from which he came, to get the tribute which the king here has owed to him for years, and it must be paid, or else the king or some one of his knights must fight with him to see whether it shall be paid or not. The black knight is such a big man and looks like such a good fighter that the men about the King seem to think it would be a pretty good thing to pay the tribute and let him go home with it. Not one of them says a word about wanting to fight with him, for a little while; but by and by, when all the rest have had a fair chance, a young man comes forward and asks the King if he may try. He is as big a man as the black knight himself, and as handsome and brave looking as any you ever dreamed of seeing, but he is so young that he cannot have fought many battles, and one would think that he would be afraid to set himself against the big black knight, unless one looked at his face, as I do, and saw that he could not possibly be afraid of anything."

"Is he braver than the one that killed the dragon?" the child asked.

"Why, no, I suppose not; nobody could be braver than he, because, you know, he could not learn what fear meant, and did not even know whether it was something to feel or something to eat or something to wear, but this young knight is just as brave as there is any need for anybody to be, and when he asks the King to let him try to beat the black knight, all the other knights say at once, 'By all means, let him try,' and they are really quite eager about it, and almost all of them change their minds about giving the tribute. So the King says that he may fight the battle if he will, and he puts on his armor, which is all of green, and mounts his horse.

"The black knight is on his horse too, and they ride far apart and then face each other and hold their long spears before them, ready for the battle. All the people stand far off at the sides, the heralds blow their trumpets, and the two knights run together with all the speed of their horses. The points of their spears are down and they are both well aimed, but each catches the other's spear fairly in the middle of his shield, and they rush together so hard that there is a great crash, and both the knights and both the horses fall to the ground with a terrible clatter of arms. But the knights are both on their feet again in a moment, and are falling upon each other with their swords, cutting and slashing and warding and advancing and retreating, till it is hard to tell which is the black knight and which the green, or whether they are not both black and both green. First one seems to be getting a little the better of the fight and then the other. The black knight is better trained, but the green knight is so much younger and fresher that he keeps his strength better, and by and by the black knight sees that he is surely gaining a little. Then he rushes upon the green knight and fights with all his strength and all his skill, and at last he gives him a wound on the shoulder. Then the green knight sees that if he is ever to do anything in this fight he must do it now, and he uses all his strength and all his skill too, and he brings down such a blow with his sword on the head of the black knight that it cuts through the helmet, and the edge of the sword is broken, and with another clash and clatter of arms the black knight falls to the ground.

"The black knight's men run to him and carry him to his ship, and sail away as quickly as they can toward their island. I can see them all the way, though it is a little dark out there, in spite of the moon, and I can see everything they do after they get there; I have to, you know, or it would spoil the story. They carry him to the King's castle, and the Queen and her daughter, who know all about medicines, and even some things that are stronger than medicines, dress his wound and nurse him and watch him day and night. But it is all of no use; nothing can cure the black knight's wound, and so he dies; but in dressing the wound the princess has found in it a little piece of steel that was broken from the edge of the green knight's sword.

"Now you ought to know, before we go any farther, that this princess is probably altogether the most beautiful princess that you ever heard a story about."

"Oh, that's the way they always are," said the little girl; "is she beautifuller than the one that had the fire all round her?"

"Perhaps not, but she was not a princess, you know; she was a goddess till her father kissed her, and then she was nothing at all till her lover came and kissed her, and after that she was a woman, which was altogether the best thing she could possibly be. But when we first saw her she was a goddess, and we have a right to expect more of her than of a princess. So I say again that this is quite the most beautiful princess that you have ever heard a story about, and you must believe it, if you please, or I shall not tell you any more about her."

"Oh, I believe anything you say," said the child, "but where is the green knight?"

"He is still here on the shore, in the King's castle, and his wound is a very bad one too, and after all the doctors have tried to cure it and have failed, one of them says that it can never be cured at all except in the country of the black knight who gave it to him. Now it is not very safe for the knight to go over to that island, where so many people would probably be glad to kill him for killing the black knight, so he disguises himself as much as he can before he goes. And he goes straight to the King's castle, just as the black knight did, and the Queen and the princess take care of him just as they took care of the black knight, only this time they have better luck, and in a little while he gets well.

"But long before he gets well the princess, who is watching by his side, sees the sword that he brought lying near by, and having nothing better to do, she looks first at the jewels in the hilt and then slowly draws the sword out of its scabbard to let her eye run along the polished blade, with its smooth, sharp edge. And then her eye quickly comes to a break in the smooth, sharp edge, and in an instant she thinks of the splinter of a sword edge that she found in her uncle's wound. At that she quickly drops the sword. Then she gets the splinter, which she has kept, and finds that it just fits the broken place in the sword, so she knows that this knight whom she is nursing and curing of his wound is the one who killed her uncle when he was fighting for her father. For a moment she thinks that she will kill him, and she lifts the sword above him, but when she sees the helpless look in his eyes she has not the heart to do it, and she lets the sword fall again. If the truth were told, I think she is already a little in love with him, and if he were any kind of knight except a green one, he would be in love with her too.

"If he only would fall in love now it might save a good deal of trouble afterwards, but because of his habit of wearing green clothes and green armor, or for some other reason, he does not, and when his wound is quite cured he sails cheerfully away again, just as if it were an everyday affair to be nursed by a queen and a princess. He sails back here to our own shore now, to the King's castle, and the King and everybody else are as glad as possible to see him. He tells them all about the Queen and the princess, and how beautiful she is, for it seems he did notice that, till by and by, when the knights of the court find that he is talking about her only in the way he would talk about a picture that pleased him, they whisper to the King that such a princess, who is so beautiful, and knows so much about curing wounds, would no doubt make a good queen, and they advise him to send for her and marry her. The green knight himself hears these whispers, and he says, 'Yes, by all means; I will go and get her; she will be glad to come, and her father and mother will be delighted to have her.' Did you ever hear of such absurd conduct from a young man dressed in green?

"Away he sails again, over to the island, and when he tells his errand the King and the Queen are delighted indeed. The princess is not so much delighted as some young women might be at the prospect of being married to a king, but she pretends to be very well pleased and says that she will go. This time it is she who makes a sad mistake, for if she would only say, right out aloud, 'I do not want to be married to this King; I want to be married to the green knight,' again it might save a good deal of trouble afterwards. She need not say it to him, but she might say it to her mother, and if he did not love her the Queen would know very well how to make him, as you shall see by and by. Still, if there were no trouble there would be no story, so we might better not complain, as long as the trouble will not be ours. So the princess sails away with the knight, and the Queen, before she goes, like a careful mother, gives her a little box of medicines such as she uses herself. That is to say, medicines and other things. One of the other things is a poison that kills anybody who drinks it, in just about a minute, and it looks and tastes just like wine. Another is a stranger mixture yet, for when a man and a woman drink it together it makes them, from that instant, love each other as long as they live, more than they love life or honor or their country or anything or anybody else in the world. And this, too, looks and tastes just like wine. It would not be easy to find two more dangerous drinks than these together.

"I see the knight and the princess now on board the ship, coming here to our shore. The knight stands near the helmsman, looking away at the sea and the sky, and thinking of nothing more sensible than how glad his King will be when he sees his bride, and how much his King will thank him for finding for him and bringing to him such a lovely princess. But the princess, who is sitting far away from him, at the other end of the ship, is thinking a great deal, and of such bitter things that she does not look at the beautiful sea and sky at all. The end of half her thoughts is that in a very little while now she will have to be the wife of a king whom she has never seen and never wants to see, because she loves the green knight, and the end of the other half of her thoughts is that she hates the knight who has brought her to this, as she could never in the world hate anybody except one whom she loved.

"And this is how her thoughts come, for you know I can see thoughts just as plainly as I can see castles and ships and battles: she thinks of her uncle, whom she loved, who fought for her father and for her country, who was wounded, and whose life she could not save; she thinks of the unknown knight who came to her, wounded too, whom she nursed and did save; she thinks how she began to love him, for the most of us love better those whom we help than those who help us; she thinks of that time when she saw his sword and knew that it was he who had killed her uncle, how her anger rose against him for that and because he had dared to come to her for help, how she had been about to kill him, and how she saw that helpless look in his eyes and had not the heart to do it. It is now that her thoughts grow bitter, for she thinks how he went away again and never dreamed of loving her for healing his wound and saving his life, and then sparing his life and loving him, when she ought to hate him and kill him, because he killed her uncle. She is beautiful enough to be loved, she thinks. Then comes a maddening thought of how this man whom she loved not only cared no more for her than for one of her father's dogs, but himself came back to ask her hand for another. This seems an insult to her and it makes her whole soul burn. She wishes she had killed him when she had his sword in her hands, and the madness fills her mind and burns her soul till she resolves that she will kill him now.

"She not only thinks all this but says it to her maid, and she orders her to take the poison out of the box of medicines that her mother gave her, and put it into a goblet, and she says that the knight shall drink some of it and that she will drink the rest herself, and so punish her enemy and be rid of the King who is to be her husband, for she will gladly die rather than be married to him. Of course this throws the poor maid into a terrible fright, for she is not a princess, and poisoning and cutting off heads, and such things seem like serious matters to her, so she would gladly save the knight and her mistress too, if she could. If you were in her place I know very well what you would do. You would give the princess some wine instead of the poison, and before she could find out what you had done, she and the knight would be on shore and would be saved. But this poor girl is so frightened that she can think of nothing to do but to give her mistress and the knight the love drink instead of the poison.

"The princess calls the knight to her and frowns upon him as dreadfully as she knows how. Can you think how a bunch of sweet, fresh, red and white roses would look if it should get terribly angry? Well, that is about the way the princess frowns. But it is not her fault. She was not made to frown. She tells the knight that he has been very cruel and very untrue to her, and that she ought to have killed him for killing her uncle; but now she says she will forgive him, and to show that they are friends she asks him to drink this wine with her. And now you may see how brave this green knight really is, for he sees well enough that she does not forgive him at all and means to kill him; yet he takes the goblet from her hand without a tremor of his own and drinks. Then she snatches the goblet from him and drinks the rest herself, and cries, 'Now we shall both die; I have my revenge upon you, and you shall not marry me to your King!'

"But, oh, it is the drink of love, and instead of dying the two stand and gaze at each other as if they could never gaze enough, then they stretch their arms toward each other, and so they meet, and now, whatever happens to either of them, they must always love each other as long as they live, more than they love life or honor or their country or anything or anybody else in the world.

"How they ever get on shore I don't know, but I do know that when they are there they make another great mistake, for they hide from the King that they love each other, and they let him think still that the princess means to be married to him, when I am sure she can mean nothing of the kind. He is a very good sort of King, who wants everybody to be as happy as possible, and he never has seen this princess before, so what can he really care for her? If they would only tell him I am sure he would be glad to help them, instead of standing in their way, but they are just as foolish as they have both been all along, and they say nothing about it.

"The princess is in the garden of the castle with her maid and they are waiting for the knight to come. The King and all his men have ridden a-hunting. It is night, and a torch burns at the castle door; at last we can see something in the fire. The knight will not come till they put out the torch, for that is the signal they have arranged, and they will not put out the torch till the hunting party is far away. You see they are still so absurdly secret about it! The maid tells the princess that she might better not put out the torch at all, for a treacherous friend of the knight has watched them, suspects their love, and has told the King; that the hunting party is only a trap, and that the King will soon come back. If it were a real hunt it would be strange for the green knight himself not to go, for he is the best huntsman in the whole country. All this is quite true; for the King, kind and generous as he is, does not like to be deceived any better than anybody else, and he wants people to keep the promises that they make to him.

"But the princess is in such haste to see the green knight again that she will not heed the maid's warning.

She sends her up to the tower to watch, as soon as she thinks the hunters are far enough away, and then she throws the torch down upon the ground and puts it out. Then the green knight comes. But they have scarcely sat down on the grassy bank to tell each other how much they love each other, and to forget all about the poor King, when the maid cries out from the tower that the huntsmen are coming back, the knight's old servant comes running with his sword drawn to his master and begs him to save himself, and in a minute they all come, the treacherous friend of the green knight leading the way, and the King next after him. The knight is standing before the princess, not thinking of himself, and the traitor, who could never match him for a moment in a fair fight, rushes upon him and wounds him, but before he can do more the King himself holds him back. The old servant raises the knight from the ground where he has fallen, drags him quickly to the shore and puts him in a ship that is there, and once more they sail away.

"The rock there by the water is no longer the castle of the King. It is the green knight's castle now, in another country, across the sea. The old servant has brought the knight here, away from his enemies, to try to heal his wound. All his care seems useless. The poor knight has all the time grown worse. But his faithful old servant has remembered who it was that cured another wound of his before, and he has sent a ship with secret messengers to bring the princess if they can. That he may know as soon as he sees the ship whether the princess is on board, he has told the sailors to hoist white sails if they bring her with them, and black sails if they do not. He is watching now for the ship to come back.

"It is the court-yard of the castle that I see, and a sweet, calm, lovely picture it is. The knight and his servant have been so long away that the place has been neglected, but it is all the prettier for that. The grass has grown long, and, as the light winds breathe upon it, it sways and sinks and rises in waves, as if it tried to be like the sea down there below it. The gray old walls and ramparts of the castle have bright green moss upon them, and from the crannies hang little plants and vines. High up, where a rough stone projects a little from the tower, a cluster of bluebells swings in the breeze and nods to the other flowers and the grass and the trees down below. Are the bluebells trying to say to the grass that up there on their airy lookout they can see away over the shining water, that the ship is not yet in sight, but that they know she will come? Beyond and away, clear to the edge of the sky, just as it is here before us now, lies the sea. Smooth and peaceful it is, as if it were resting all through this calm day. Over it all the sun is sending a flood of light, fifty times as bright as the light of this splendid moon of ours. But now and then it is dimmed a little, for far away on the sea lies a strip of shade, the shadow of a cloud; slowly it moves toward the land, as the cloud sails through the blue sky, and as it comes it is seen plainer and moves faster, till the shadow reaches the shore and rests for an instant on the castle and the court-yard, and then it passes away into the land and everything is sunny again.

"Yet in all this light and peaceful beauty there is something that seems like sadness. In the court-yard, on his couch, lies the knight, in the cool shade. He does not know where he is, and he does not know his servant, who stands beside him, with the tears in his faithful old eyes, but he must know that he is in a beautiful place. Does everything in the place know that he is here, too, and feel sad to see him lying sick and wounded and weak and weary? The sun veils his face oftener than he does on some of our bright days, and when there is no cloud he shines with a soft, mellow light, the sea throws shades of purple over its blue and silver, and its waves break against the shore with only a soft little sound, and a sort of hushed song that is like a moan and is like a lullaby too. You can hear it down there among the pebbles around the rock. The bluebells swing softly, as if they were afraid to ring out aloud and disturb the sleeping knight. The hard walls look softer for their coverings of moss; the grass waves slowly and bends toward the wounded man, seeming to listen to his breathing. A shepherd leans over the rampart and plays a soft, sad, sleepy little air on his pipe. 'Is the knight awake?' he calls to the servant.

"'No,' the servant answers, 'and unless the princess comes I fear he will never wake; watch for the ship.'

"'I will watch,' the shepherd says, 'and if I see the ship I will play a lively tune on my pipe to tell you of it.'

"The knight begins to wake and stir; he asks where he is, and the servant tells him that he is at his own castle. He has been dreaming of the princess, and the servant says, 'I have sent the ship for her; she will come to-day.' But the knight is so weak that he cannot understand or talk of one thing very long, and he falls half asleep again and dreams of the princess, and because he has heard of a ship he dreams of other ships. He has his old wound now and is lying, just as he lies here, in that ship which bore him the first time toward the princess; now she is with him and his face grows lighter. She is looking at his sword; she raises it again, as she did so long ago, to kill him; but she sees again the helpless look in his eyes and has not the heart to do it, and she lets the sword fall again. He is on a second ship, sailing toward the princess to bring her for the King's bride; now the ship is sailing back and they are together on the deck. She holds out to him that goblet of strange wine; they both drink, they gaze into each other's eyes, the dream is too happy to last, and he awakes and cries, 'Has the ship come? Can you not see her yet?'

"'Not yet,' the servant answers; 'but she must come soon.'

"The knight is in the garden of the castle - the other castle - waiting for the princess to put out the torch, hat he may come to her. The torch falls upon the ground, he runs toward the place, and they are together yet again. It is another happy dream that cannot stay. 'Is the ship nowhere in sight?'

"Before the servant can answer he hears the merry tune from the shepherd's pipe and knows that the ship is coming now, indeed. He looks away across the sea and tells his master how swiftly it flies over the water toward them, with its white sails, for the sails are white and the princess is on board. The time seems long to the knight and his servant, yet it is really short, for the wind is fair. The ship comes nearer and nearer, it passes the dangerous reef, it is so near that the servant can see the faces of the princess and the helmsman and the sailors. Now it is at the very shore and the princess is at the gate. Ah, it was not medicines that the knight needed. With the very knowledge that the princess is there, he raises himself from his couch and walks toward the gate. Then his little strength fails again and he would fall, but the princess herself catches him in her arms and holds him. This time it is no dream.

"She leads him back to the couch, he sinks upon it, and she bends over him. But suddenly the shepherd runs to the rampart and cries that another ship is coming, the King's ship. Are the King's men coming then to carry back the princess, perhaps to kill the knight? The servant calls the men of the castle and they try to barricade and guard the gate. But they are too late; the King's men and the King himself break through the barriers and are in the courtyard. The very first of them is the knight's treacherous friend; the old servant instantly cuts him down with his sword, and there is one good stroke at least. Then the King calls to all to hold their hands and to strike no more; he has come only to give the princess to the knight. He has heard of the love drink, and knows at last that they were not to blame for what they did, and that they never meant to be false to him.

"But still the knight lies there on his couch and the princess kneels by his side and bends over him, and neither of them speaks or moves."

"And will the knight get well again?" the little girl asked.

"Let us not try to find out any more now," I said. "The knight and the princess are both here, and I know that they are happier together than they have ever been before. That is enough, is it not?"

All at once there were voices behind us, three voices at least.

"Hello, there! who's attending to the fire? You're letting it all go out, and there's plenty of wood left."

"What are you two doing here all alone? Don't you know you'll catch your death o' cold sitting here so long?"

"Are there any marshmallows left?"

"No," said the little girl, answering the last question, "we don't care about marshmallows any way," and I really believe just then she thought she did not care about them, though usually she likes them almost as well as anybody.

THE MINSTREL KNIGHT

The little girl stayed at the seashore till the middle of the autumn. That is the way sensible people do, when they can, and I have worked much in vain if I have not shown by this time that this little girl is a sensible little person. The spring is very lovely, to be sure, and of course we all love it. I should be the last one to say anything against it. But to me the most beautiful time of the whole beautiful year is the early autumn. The heat and the work and the worry of the year are over, and the clear, rich, golden good of it all is left to be enjoyed. The flowers are not pink and pale blue any more; they are of deep, splendid yellow and red and purple. The golden-rod and the asters are lords of flowers, and the cardinal is their high-priest, while if you will have something that is delicate and modest, there is the fringed gentian, and that shows, too, how healthy and brave and free it is by keeping no company with dark shadows, and opening only when the bright sun shines full upon it.

But of the things that are best in the autumn, the best above all others is the sea. It has been lying quiet and restful all summer, and now it awakes and begins to move and to show the strength and the freedom of its glorious life. As you stand upon the shore and look at it, it draws itself away from you and away from the land as if it were done with it forever; then it pauses, and in a moment begins to come back. Up and up the beach it marches with a majestic will that nothing else in the world is like; as it comes it lifts itself higher and higher; then the wave leaps into the air and its crest is turned to emerald as the sunlight strikes through it for the pause of another instant, there is a roll, a mad plunge, the spray dashes high above your head, the foam floats and flies up the beach to your very feet, the hollow rumble of the water sounds fainter and farther along the sands, and the ocean draws itself back away from you and away from the land. Its colors are different, too. Before it had all sorts of fanciful hues and shades, pale green and blue, silver, violet, almost rose sometimes, the colors of summer dreams. Now the dreaming time is over. The green of the wave-crests is luminous, the white and the blue have the gleam of polished steel, the violet and the rose are turned to deep, rich purple. The sea is not cold, harsh, and cruel yet, but it is free, bold, and majestic.

All this I knew because I remembered it, not because I saw it, for I had been back in the city a long time. The fire was lighted again and I had sat before it often, thinking of the driftwood fire away down there, with the little girl sitting before it, seeing pictures in it for herself, perhaps, and listening to the low sound of the sea, coming up through the still evening air. But one night she came and sat with me again, and once more we both looked into the same fire. "I believe I can almost see pictures myself now," she said.

"Can you? And what do you see in the fire now?"

"Oh, I can see a prince and a princess - and a knight - and a lovely goddess, like the one that had the apples - and a cave, like the one where the dragon lived - "

"And don't you see the dragon himself? Where is he?"

"No, there isn't any dragon; that would be too much like the other story."

"But you must not mind that. There are only a few good stories altogether, and the most we can do, as I told you once before, is to tell them over and over again in different ways."

"But I don't want any dragon in this one. Now you tell me what they all do, the goddess and the knight, and the prince and the princess, and what the cave is for."

"Very well, I will try. First I see the knight. He is riding along upon his horse, through the forests, over the hills and across the valleys. It is a lovely day of summer. When he comes to the top of a hill, he sees the country lying before him and all around him, deep green with woods and pastures and paler green where the grain is ripening. Here and there, too, it is sprinkled with tiny dots of red, where the poppies grow thick in a field, and there are spots that are almost blue with cornflowers. A silver ribbon of a river winds through it, and the sight of it is lost among the blue mountains. As he rides down into a valley the branches wave above him and break the sunshine that falls upon the road and the grass beside it. The flecks of light and the patches of shade tremble and waver and dart across and across the way, as if they were weaving a robe for the earth, of gold and brown and green. The air is full of the smell of the flowers, a brook makes a soft, cheery little noise, and from the pastures comes the sleepy sound of sheep-bells.

"The knight is riding toward the castle of the prince.

He is a minstrel, as well as a knight, and at the castle he will meet other minstrels who are his friends, and they are all to sing for a prize which the prince has offered. There is as much happiness in the heart of the knight as in everything around him, for he loves the prince's daughter, and he knows that she loves him. Besides this she is to give the prize to the one who wins it, and with his mind full of gladness and thoughts of her, he feels sure that he can win.

"As he rides thus the evening falls. The moon comes up, and from the hills the country stretches darkly away all around, with the silver ribbon of the river still winding through it. The shade is so deep in the valleys that he has to ride through them slowly. The robe of the earth now is all of deep gray and silver. The smell of the flowers is stronger and sweeter than before, the brooks sound louder, and the sheep bells are silent. The knight's thoughts just now are wandering away from the princess, and he is thinking of the fame that he hopes to win as a minstrel, how he will gain this prize and many other prizes, how kings will send for him to come to their courts, that they may hear his songs, how he will grow great and rich, and how his name will live on after he is dead.

"As he thinks of these things, suddenly he sees a strange form before him in the valley. It is like a woman, wonderfully beautiful, marvellously, magically beautiful. Something more than the moonlight seems to rest upon her and to show him her face with its deep eyes and soft cheeks, her movements, so graceful and gentle that it seems as if she did not move herself at all, but were just stirred and swayed by the little breezes. A rosy light shines from her face and around her dark hair. All about her are nymphs, or fairies, dancing and gliding and scattering roses for her to walk upon. It seems really quite needless to do that, for she appears rather to float and move in the air and to rest on the flower-perfumed wind than to stand or walk upon the ground. Now a knight who was also a minstrel could not possibly make any mistake about such a person as this, and he knows at once that she is the very Goddess of Love and Beauty."

"Is she the one that had the apples?" the little girl asked.

"No, not quite the same. She is one something like her, yet a good deal different."

"Is she Venus then?"

"Yes, you have guessed just right, and so at last somebody in our story has a name. But she is not altogether like the Venus that you have heard about so many times before. Some people used to believe that after the old gods whom you know so well had lost their rule on Mount Olympus, they went to live inside the mountains and under the ground, and that they were not kind to men any more, but always did harm, whenever they were able to do anything. Now, for myself, I don't quite see how this could be, because you know we have felt so sure that we saw some of them up in the sky sometimes. Yet now that I see Venus here, it does seem to me as if there were something in the story after all, and I believe it would be better for the knight if he had never seen her at all. If he were thinking of the princess at the time I do not believe he would look twice at Venus. No, I am sure he would not even see her once.

"But since he is not thinking of the princess, but only of what a great man he would be if he could make his songs seem as wonderful to everybody else as they seem to himself, it is not surprising that he is delighted by such a vision, and it is not surprising, either, when the goddess and her nymphs beckon to him and then glide away as if they wanted him to follow them, that he gets off his horse and does follow them. They move along so fast that he cannot keep up with them, and soon he cannot even see them, but it is still easy for him to follow. For everywhere they go the strangest flowers spring up under their feet and make a pathway to lead him. They are huge, bright flowers, cup-shaped and star-shaped and sun-shaped. Flowers of such wonderful form and size, and such gorgeous colors the knight never saw before. Some of them seem to be made of hammered gold, and some of silver; some have stamens of precious stones, and some look like clear crystal, blood-red, deep purple, or orange, as if they were cut from solid gems; some of them have petals like flames, that shimmer and glow and are reflected by the others; the leaves are all glistening emerald and they are sprinkled with pearls like drops of evening dew. The stems twine about like serpents, and they seem to the knight to move and turn about to show him all their magic splendor. Some of them, with coiling tendrils, like gold wire, sway toward him as if they would catch him and hold him, others dance and wave about on their stems and twinkle as the other stars do, up above the trees, as if they were laughing and mocking at him, and still others bow and bend away from him and beckon him on. The whole of the fire is scarcely enough to show me this strange garden. A pale, ghostly light rises from all the flowers and hovers over the path. The knight would stop to pick some of them, but those before him seem always more beautiful than those close at hand, and, besides, he is eager to follow the goddess. So on he hurries till he sees before him a way straight into the side of the mountain and within a great glare of light. If he would only think of the princess now, for one instant! But he goes straight on into the mountain, and the way shuts behind him, and outside the magic flowers are gone, and there is nothing but the soft grass, the whispering trees, the dark sky, with the stars, and the calm night.

"Do you see how very wrong it is for the knight to go away after the goddess into the mountain? When people let themselves be led away like that by fairies and goddesses it is usually a long time before they get back. A knight like this one, who is a minstrel as well, ought to know all about such things, and I dare say he does. He must have heard of men who went to such places and saw beautiful and wonderful sights, and feasted and danced till they thought that they had been away from their homes for a day, or a week, and then, when they went back to them, found that they had really been gone for years, perhaps for hundreds of years, and that all their friends were dead. He ought to think of his friends, the other knights and minstrels, who will be grieved when they meet and he is not with them. For his own sake he ought to know better than to run into strange and dangerous places just because they look pleasant. More than all, he ought to think of the princess. If he does not care for the prize of his song any more for itself he should care for her who is to give it. He should remember how much she loves him, little as he deserves it. She will not forget him as he does her. When she waits and waits for him and he does not come she will believe that he is dead, and she will cry her pretty eyes out. She will never think that he has gone away from her to visit a goddess of love and beauty who lives in a cave.

"Now I see the cave of the goddess, deep in the mountain. It seems dim and misty and confused at first, but gradually I can see it clearer. All around the sides and the top are great pendants of gems, like icicles, of all sorts of colors, as if the precious stones had once been liquid and had run down into the cave and then had frozen into crystal. Here and there are diamonds and rubies and opals and emeralds as big as your head, set in the roof, and they have some magical way of shining all by themselves and light up the whole cave like lamps. The ground is covered with flowers like those that made the path to lead the knight to the place. A stream of water runs from the cave and is fed by fountains in the middle. These fountains are wonderful affairs too. Sometimes they throw jets of liquid silver almost to the roof; then they fall down and spread out wide in sheets, of the color and the brightness of melted gold; again the water rises in little streams that twine and weave themselves together like basket-work, and all of deep, shining crimson; then the fountains take other fantastic forms and other colors, purple or green or orange, but always glowing with light, and so they pass to silver and to gold again.

"This is the cave of Venus. It is filled with the nymphs who attend her, and they are singing choruses in her praise, and dancing wonderful, mazy, mad, delirious dances. They whirl about and around alone, in couples, in lines, in circles, and in crowds, their arms waving and their hair streaming in the air. Sometimes while they dance every one is plainly to be seen, and again their garments surround them like clouds, and they are all one waving, streaming, fluttering mass. These mists of light robes then are like the fountains, for now they are shining white, now red or yellow or green or purple, now all the colors together, mixed and blended like broken and tangled rainbows.

"If you could see all that I see here in the fire I think you would be delighted with it, for a little while. But how do you suppose the minstrel knight likes it? He sits beside the goddess and looks at it wearily. He has seen them all so much that walls of gems and streams of gold and whirling rainbows do not please him any more. He has been here in the cave for a whole year. He sees now how wrong it was for him to come, and he is so tired of it all that he is beginning to feel that he would rather die than be among these mad pleasures any longer. But he cannot do that because nobody ever dies here. When he sees these walls of cold crystal, gleaming with the colored light from the great gems, he thinks of the broad, lovely country that he once saw, that stretched away and ended only at the blue mountains, and of the silver river that never changed to blood, or to green fire, with the clear sunlight brightening them all.

"If he tries to rest his eyes upon the great, glowing, magic flowers that cover the ground, they only make him think of the red poppies that shone out from the fields of ripening grain, and of the blue of the cornflowers, and then he tries to think of the perfume from the flowers that filled the air after it grew still at evening. There are odors here, too, but they are so heavy and sweet that after a time it is almost a pain to smell them. He hears the rush and the dash of the fountains, and he longs for the low, merry little sound of the brook that ran along beside his road. The air here is full of music, the rich harmonies of many instruments and the voices of the nymphs who sing their choruses to Venus, but his ears are tired of the sounds, and he wishes that he might hear only the sleepy tinkle of the sheep-bells, chiming with the voice of the brook. But more than everything else he thinks of the princess. He remembers now how kind and true she was, and how much truer he ought to have been in return than he really was. He wonders if she still remembers him, if she thinks him dead, and then his heart stops, as he wonders if she herself is dead. Oh, it is a fine time now to think of these things! If he had only remembered the princess once before, instead of thinking what a great minstrel he was, he would never have followed Venus into her cave. Now he can only think of that great wrong he did and long for the fresh fields and woods, for the air, the sunlight - and the princess.

"Venus, sitting by his side, sees that he is troubled and asks him why. He tells her how much he wishes that he might see again the world he used to know, and live the life he used to live, and he begs her to let him go. She is angry at first. Has she not brought him to live here among such delights as no man before ever knew, and is he tired of them now, and does he want to escape from them? He can only say that he will never forget her or the beautiful things he has seen here, but he can never be happy here again, and if she will only let him he must go. At last she tells him that he may go. 'But you will not be happy,' she says; 'your old friends will scorn you when they know where you have been. They will never forgive you for coming here. You will find no rest, no help, no hope. Then, when you learn that you can have peace nowhere else, come back to me and stay with me forever.'

"All at once the cave, with everything in it, is gone.

The knight knows how or where it went no more than I. As for him, he does not know that he has moved from his place, and as for me, the fire is burning just as it did before. Yet now I see him lying on the soft grass of a beautiful valley. Above him are the sky and the nodding branches of the trees; around are the hills. He sees and he smells the flowers that were lost to him so long. The low tinkle of the sheep-bells comes again drowsily to his ears. A little way up the hill a shepherd is playing softly on his pipe. He picks a flower and smells it, to be sure that it is all real. Then the tears come to his eyes as he thinks of all the beauty and sweetness of the life that he lost and has found again.

"But now a band of pious pilgrims passes, on the way to Rome. They are going to ask the Pope to forgive their sins. The sight of them brings a new thought to the knight. It is the thought of his own sin. Now that he sees again the sweet loveliness of the world, he feels at last fully how wicked it was for him to leave it and all his own duties and his friends in it. He is in despair when he thinks that he is no longer worthy of the princess, if indeed he ever were. He dares not see her again; he dares not ask his friends to be his friends longer; he throws himself upon the ground and feels that he has no more a place in this happy world.

"At this very moment comes a company of huntsmen riding past. Their leader is the prince himself and the rest are the friends of the minstrel knight, the very ones with whom he should have sung for the prize a year ago. Very glad they are to find him, after thinking him dead so long, and they insist that he must come with them and be one of them again. He will not go with them. He feels that he is not like them any more. His wrong has been so great that he dares not be with brave, good men. They urge him, but it is useless. But there is one among them, a knight and a minstrel too, who also loves the princess. She does not love him, but his own love is so deep and true that he will do anything to make her happy. When he finds that nothing else can move the stubborn knight he tells him that the princess still loves him, that she has grieved for him all the time that he has been lost, and that he must come back to them for her sake. He is touched at last. He had not dared to ask of her, and now he knows that he may see her again, that she could never forget like him, that she will love him and forgive him. He cannot resist. He will go.

"They are all in the hall of the prince's castle now. They are to sing again for a prize and again the princess is to give it. The prince tells them that they must all sing of love. The knight who loves the princess hopelessly begins. He sings of his own love, how it is fixed upon one who does not love him in return, and how still his love for her is all the joy he has, and he would gladly lose the last blood of his heart for her. They all cry out that he has sung nobly, except the knight from the cave of Venus. He thinks this is a very weak, silly kind of love; he sings in a very different way, and he tells them that if they want to know what love really is they must go and learn of the Goddess of Love.

"They are all filled with horror. They know now where he has been. He has left the princess for Venus; he has learned to scorn their knightly love; worse than all, it seems to them, he, a Christian man, has passed a whole year in the home of a heathen goddess. They declare that he has betrayed them in daring to come among them like an honest knight. They forget that he refused to come, that he told them he was unworthy of them and was too wicked to be one of them, and they almost compelled him. So their swords are out to kill him. But the princess, whom he has injured a thousand times as much as all of them put together, commands them to spare him. He may yet be forgiven, she says, and it is not for them to judge. She will pray for him as long as she lives, and God may pardon him. At her word they draw back and put up their swords, yet they think his guilt too great ever to be forgiven. There can be but one only hope for him, says the prince; some of the pilgrims on their way to Rome are still in the valley; he must go with them and pray for pardon from the Pope.

"Never another pilgrim toiled along the road to Rome feeling such a heavy weight of sin to be forgiven as the minstrel knight. He does not talk with the others or lighten the way as they do with holy songs. He knows not how to suffer enough for his guilt, and to seek out punishments for himself is his only content. Some of the pilgrims walk where the grass is soft and cool; he chooses the paths that are full of stones and thorns. They drink at the springs of cold water; he thirsts more than they, but he turns away and lets the noon sun blaze down upon his bare head. They find shelter and rest for the night; he lies upon the snow of the mountain and sleeps there, if he sleeps at all. When he comes near to Italy he fears that the sight of that lovely land will be pleasing to his eyes, and so he has himself led blindfold on to Rome.

"The Pope sits upon his throne, and before him come all who seek for pardon. He forgives them, blesses them, and sends them away. At last comes the minstrel knight. He throws himself on the stones before the feet of the Pope and tells the story of all the wrong that he has done. The Pope listens and is filled with horror, as the prince and the knights were before, and there is no princess here to say one word of love or mercy. 'There is no hope for you,' he answers, 'no pardon, no hope. Your guilt is too deep and black. As soon shall this naked staff I hold bear flowers and leaves as one like you find forgiveness or mercy.'

"And so the minstrel knight shrinks away. He knows not where to turn. All places are alike to him, alike full of darkness and despair. The pilgrims are returning home. He follows them, as a dog that had been struck and wounded might crawl after men who had been his friends.

"I see the beautiful valley again. The princess is kneeling before a little cross. She is praying that the knight whom she loves may be forgiven. Back in the rising shadows of the evening stands the knight who loves her hopelessly, watching her as she prays. The pilgrims are coming from Rome. They are singing songs of mercy and peace. The princess looks eagerly among them. The minstrel knight is not there. 'He will never come back,' she sighs, and she turns away and slowly climbs the hill toward her father's castle, where she may pray for him again.

"And now a dark figure comes slowly, fearfully on, by the way that the pilgrims have passed. He sees his friend, standing where he stood while the princess prayed. He calls to him to stand back; he is too guilty for any good man to touch or come near him. He tells him how he went to Rome and what the Pope said. Then he tells the awful thought that is now in his mind. The Goddess of Love and Beauty bade him when all hope should be lost to come to her again and stay with her forever. He is seeking her mountain now. He calls to her to guide him. Now at the very back of the fire I see a rising red glow. The goddess is there and she calls to him to hasten to her. 'You are mad,' cries his friend; 'stay; be brave; bear it all, and you may yet be forgiven.'

"Suddenly there comes to the knight another thought - the best thought he has ever had - the princess. Instantly the red glow is gone and the goddess is hidden from him forever. His friend knows his thought. 'She is up there,' he says, 'praying for you still.'

"At last the knight is humbled, overcome, subdued. He falls upon his face and prays for pardon, as the princess is praying for him up there in the castle. And now all at once there is a glad shout, a song of happiness and peace. Another band of pilgrims has come from Rome. They are bringing the staff of the Pope, and all in a night it has borne flowers and leaves. The smell of lilies fills the air. They are carrying the staff through the land to tell the knight and all other men like him, if, indeed, there are others, that they are forgiven. The minstrel knight has found pardon and he may rest."

"And what became of the princess?" the little girl asked.

"The fire is too low," I said; "I cannot see any more. What do you think became of her?"

"I don't know," she answered, "but I think she must be very happy that the knight is forgiven."

"I think they are both very happy," I said.

THE KING OF THE GRAIL

It was the last evening of the year. In honor of the occasion the little girl was allowed to sit up rather later than usual - not till midnight, of course, so that she could see how different the whole world would look after the clock had struck, but long enough to make her feel that she was doing something very pleasant, because something that it was not good for her to do very often. Our friends down by the sea had sent us a strange Christmas present, but they knew what we wanted. It was a big box of driftwood, almost a wagon-load. We resolved that it should not be used except on great occasions, and of course New Year's eve was a great occasion. Here in the city we could not listen in the evening stillness and catch the low murmur of the restless water, but the fire burned with the same strange and lovely colors as if it had been kindled on the beach. Tonight it was not likely that we should see any storms or any ghostly ships, yet the little girl knew well enough that there were wonderful things to be seen in that fire.

"What can you see in it?" I asked her.

"I don't want to see things myself," she said. "I want you to see them. Just think; this is the last time we can have any stories about the fire this year."

"But the new year will begin to-morrow," I said, "and it will be just as good as the old one, will it not?"

"Oh, yes, I suppose so," she said, "but this has been such a nice year that I don't like to have it go. But now tell me what is in the fire."

"There are so many strange things in it that I scarcely know how to begin to tell you about them. I am very much afraid that I shall not make you understand all that I see in the fire to-night, and I am the more afraid of it because I am not at all sure that I can quite understand it all myself. But first the reddest and brightest spot in the whole fire begins to grow redder and brighter and to take a new shape. It is the shape of a goblet. It is of clear crystal and its sharp angles and edges sparkle with many colors, but within it that strange, deep red glows and shines and grows brighter still, till it beats and throbs as if it were alive. And all around it, too, there is a circle of soft rays of light, like a halo.

"Perhaps you know what this is, but I am afraid you don't Do you remember what I told you once about the Holy Grail? This is the Holy Grail - the cup from which the Saviour drank at the Last Supper, and in which afterwards His blood was caught as He hung upon the cross. It is that blood in the cup which is still alive and glows and beats and throbs. This Holy Grail, as I told you before, is guarded by a band of knights in a beautiful temple, which nobody can find except those whom the Grail itself has chosen and allowed to come. I can see the temple now. It has a high, light, graceful dome, which rests on tall pillars of marble that is like snow. The whole temple may be of something like snow, too, for it melts away so that I cannot see it and comes again, then half of it is gone and then the other half, so that I scarcely know whether I see it at all. Perhaps it is the smoke of the fire that makes it seem so. But I can see that the dome is all covered with figures and traceries of gold, which bloom out bright like flowers whenever the whole dome looks plainest, and then fade again. But when the smoke comes across the whole picture and darkens it for a moment, then the lines upon the dome show through it like fire, and they change and waver, and then the whole temple is gone again.

"You remember something about the Grail's knights. The Knight of the Swan was one of them. They live here in the temple, except when they are sent away on some journey, to help some one who is in trouble, to do some act of justice, to fight for the right, or to punish the wrong. And whether they stay here or go as far away as they can, they never need any food except what the Grail gives them. The Grail chooses them at first, feeds them afterwards, and gives them their commands, for sometimes, in that halo that shines around it, there appear letters and words to tell the knights what they should know. And once a year, on Good Friday, a white dove flies into the temple and rests upon the Holy Grail, to give it more of these powers for the coming year.

"I see now a strange-looking man with a dark face and deep, bright eyes which seem never to rest, but always to look and search for something that they never find. Yet now and then a cruel light comes into them and makes them blaze for an instant, and his hard lips smile a little, and then his face grows stern and gloomy again. He is a wicked magician. Once he wanted to join the Knights of the Grail. He could even be their king, he thought. But the Grail chose its own knights and it did not choose him. Then he swore that he would be avenged upon the Grail knights; he would tempt them away from the temple, he would overthrow them, he would find a way to steal the Grail itself. It was for this that he learned his magic. He built an enchanted castle not far from the Temple of the Grail and filled it with every kind of pleasure that he could devise. Then he tried to entice good knights to come to his castle, and if any knight came, if any stayed in the enchanted halls to eat or drink or dance or play, that knight was lost forever. He could go back to his old friends and his old life no more, and his use in the world was ended.

"Again I see a woman - a woman yet more strange than this man. You will think so when I tell you who she is. You remember the wife of the King, whose daughter danced before the King and pleased him so much that he promised her any gift she should ask; how the Queen told her to ask for the head of the great prophet, who was in prison, and how the head was cut off and brought to her. This woman whom I see was that Queen. The old stories say that she saw the Saviour as He passed, bearing His cross upon His back, and that she laughed at Him. He only looked at her sorrowfully and spoke no word. But always from that time she was forced to wander through the world, and laugh at everything that was true and good. Can you think of anything more horrible? After a long, weary time she wished that she might die, but still through all lands she journeyed, laughing at everything she saw that was sweet and pure and holy. The wish to die grew and grew till it was her only longing. But she could not die. For hundreds of years she has lived unchanged. Some say that she can never die or grow old till the best knight of all the world shall come and pardon her great sins. Others say that she must live till one comes whom she cannot tempt away by her beauty from the path he follows.

"For she is very beautiful. It is not the beauty of a common woman that she has, but something far beyond it. She can be tender, sweet, gentle, enticing, and then in an instant proud, defiant, radiant. Perhaps the wicked magician has given her some of this wonderful beauty by his magic, for she is in his power and helps him to entrap knights into his castle, where they lose all hope of returning to the life of the world and of doing good in it. She does not wish to do this, but the magician compels her. So always she must tempt and entice at his command the knights who come near his castle, and always she must long for one to come whom she cannot tempt, for then she will be free. The knights of the Grail are not the men for whom she waits. To tempt them is only too easy. Even their King cannot resist her.

"I see the King of the Grail now. He holds a spear in his hand that is almost as great and wonderful a thing as the Grail itself. From the point of the spear flows a little stream of blood. It trickles down the shaft of the spear to the King's hand that holds it, but the blood does not stain the hand; it flows over it and leaves it clean and white. It is the very spear with which the Roman soldier wounded the side of the Saviour, and ever since that time the blood has run from its point. But the King has wandered too far away from the Temple of the Grail and too near the magician's enchanted castle. The magician sees him and sends the woman to try to bring him within his power. Such wonderful beauty as hers the King has never seen before. For one instant in looking at her he forgets to guard the spear; he lets it go from his hand, the magician seizes it and strikes the King with it in the side. He is borne back to the temple with just such a wound as that other which this same spear made so many years ago. And the magician has the spear. As he holds it the blood flows from its point and trickles down the shaft, and as it flows over his hand it stains it a deep, ugly red. He carries the spear to his castle. He has stolen this, and now he will wait on and watch for a chance to steal the Grail.

"And the wound in the King's side will not heal. All that can be done with medicines and balsams and ointments is done, but they are of no use. Many years pass - yes, just while we are looking into the fire - and still the wound is the same, still it burns and stings, and still it bleeds again whenever the King uncovers the Grail so that it may feed the knights who are in the temple and help those who are far away. Some wounds, some sicknesses, the Grail itself can cure, but it cannot cure this, or it will not. Yet once, while the King knelt before it, he saw words that shone like fire in the halo around it, and they said: 'Wait for the simple Fool, taught by pity, for him I have chosen.' Perhaps you do not see quite what that means. Well, I don't think the King quite knows what it means either, but he knows that he has something to wait for, and that is better than knowing nothing at all about it. That was years ago, and still the wound burns and stings, and still it bleeds when the King uncovers the Grail.

"When we look into the fire we can go back through the years just as well as forward. So now, going back for a little while and far away from the Temple of the Grail, I see something very different from what we have seen before. I see a boy who lives with his mother in a forest. His father was a knight and was killed in battle. His mother feared that when he grew up he would want to be a knight too, and would be killed in the same way, so she brought him here to the forest and kept him away from the great world where men live and work and fight, and never let him know anything about knights or battles or tournaments or the courts of kings. She lets him learn to shoot with a bow as he grows up, and to hunt the beasts of the woods. He can hit any bird that flies with his arrows, and he runs so fast that he can catch the deer by the horns.

"Yet he does not know that men wear armor and fight with spears and swords, and he has never heard of an army or a battle. Perhaps he may be almost enough of a simple fool about these things to help the King of the Grail."

"I don't think he was a fool at all," said the little girl, "if his mother wouldn't let him hear anything about such things."

"I think," I answered, "that the letters around the Grail could not have meant quite what we mean by a fool. The Grail would not choose any such person, I am sure. They must have meant some one who was good and simple and had not learned the ways of the world. And then you know the letters said, 'taught by pity,' so I suppose he is to be a fool at all only till he is 'taught by pity.' Well, the mother might have known that she could not keep her boy in this ignorance forever, and so one day he meets three knights riding through the forest. He is filled with wonder and delight at their polished armor, their waving plumes, and their long spears, with their glittering points. He asks them who they are and what all these wonderful things are for. They tell him that they are knights, and everything else that he wants to know, and then he runs home to his mother and tells her that he wants to go away and see the world and be a knight too.

"She tries to tell him that knights are wicked men, but he will not believe it, and he begs her to let him go. She sees that she cannot keep him, that all her care has been lost, and at last she says that he may go. He has no armor, but perhaps he may get that some time. He takes his bow and his arrows and wanders away through the forest, and his mother looks after him till she can see no more through her tears.

"We are back near the Temple of the Grail now. I see a beautiful, deep forest. An old knight and two young squires are lying on a green bank and are just awaking at the sound of trumpets from the temple. They are scarcely awake when a strange creature is seen coming toward them. It is a woman upon a galloping horse. And the horse is strange enough too. Its mane is so long that it drags upon the ground, and then the wind catches it and blows it about till the horse looks like a hurrying black cloud, and its eyes show through the cloud like flashes of lightning. The woman's eyes sometimes are deep and full of fire, and sometimes they look dull and cold, almost dead. She is not beautiful. She has a dark face, burned as if she had travelled much under hot suns. Her long black hair is in disorder and flies all about her in the wind. Her dress is in disorder too, and it is fastened around the waist by a girdle of snake skin, with long ends that hang down to the ground. Everything about her looks wild and terrible. She is a woman whom you would not care to meet on a lonely road after dark and on a horse like this. Yet if you looked at her face more closely you would not find anything cruel in it, but you would find a great deal of sorrow and suffering.

"You can never guess who this woman is, so I must tell you. She is the very same who helps the wicked magician to entice knights into his castle. She looks very different now, to be sure, but it is a strange life that she leads altogether. It is only when she is asleep that the magician has power over her. When she is awake she tries to atone a little for her great sins by serving the Holy Grail. She rides all over the world and brings news of battles or messages from knights of the Grail who are in distant countries, or she stays here and finds work to do at home. But always, because of her curse, she laughs, even at the good that she herself tries to do. And at last the longing for rest comes upon her again till she cannot resist it. She sinks to sleep, and then the magician calls her. She is forced to obey him, he gives her back that wonderful beauty, and she helps him in his wicked work.

"Now she has been all the way to Arabia to find a balsam for the King's wound. She gives it to the old knight, in a little flask, and then throws herself upon the ground to rest. At the same time there comes a train of knights, bearing the King of the Grail in a litter toward the lake for his morning bath. He thanks the woman for bringing the balsam, but she only laughs at what she has done and at his thanks. It will do him no good, she says. Alas, he knows too well that it will do him none. Nobody can do him good but the simple Fool, taught by pity. And so they carry him on to his bath.

"The old knight stays behind. 'Why should we try all

these things,' he thinks again, 'when none can help him but the simple Fool?' At this instant a swan flies up from the lake and then suddenly flutters and falls upon the ground. There is an arrow through its heart. Everybody who sees it cries out in horror, for it is one of the laws of this place that no animal shall be harmed. What man cruel enough to kill this beautiful, harmless swan can have found his way here, where none can come who is not chosen by the Grail? In a moment some squires run in, bringing the murderer of the swan. He is scarcely a man at all, hardly more than a boy, and he carries a bow and arrow. It is the same boy whom we saw living in the woods with his mother. The old knight looks at him sorrowfully. 'Did you kill this poor bird?' he asks.

"'Yes, to be sure,' says the young man,' I can hit anything.'

"The old knight talks with him kindly and tells him how wrong it is to kill harmless things. His mother never taught him that. She only tried to keep him from knowing anything about knights. The old man makes him see how cruel he has been, and at last the boy throws away his arrows and breaks his bow. Now the knight asks him who he is, whence he comes, and who was his father, but he can answer nothing. Indeed, he knows little enough of these things, for his mother never told him. His mother and the life that he led with her in the forest are all that he can remember to tell the old knight. Even of his mother and of his old life the strange woman who lies upon the grass can tell more than he, for she has seen him and his mother often, though they did not see her, and she laughs at the poor woman who thought she could keep her son from ever knowing anything of arms and battles. She tells him, too, that his mother is dead; she saw her die as she passed, because he had left her. The boy is moved at last, frightened, bewildered. He never knew anybody but his mother; she was his only friend; she taught him all he ever learned; and she is dead because of him. What shall he do now?

"The King and his train come back again from the lake and pass on toward the temple. The woman feels the terrible weariness coming upon her again. She struggles against it, but it is of no use. She sinks upon the ground behind the low bushes and sleeps. The magician can have her now if he wants her, and surely he will want her.

"The old knight has been watching the boy. 'Can it be,' he thinks, 'that this is the Fool, taught by pity, for whom we were to wait?' That he is a fool the old man thinks is clear enough, but how could he kill the swan? He cannot have been taught very much by pity. But perhaps the time for that has not come yet, and surely he could not get here at all if the Grail had not chosen him in some way. Perhaps if he sees the King, so pale and sick with his wound, and knows how he has suffered with it these many years, he may be moved to pity and may learn some needful things. So the old knight leads him gently away toward the Temple of the Grail.

"They walk through the forest and among the rocks, and as they go there comes to them a sound of chimes. It grows clearer as they go on, till they reach the temple, and then it is over their heads. They are in a grand, beautiful hall that is something like a church, but not quite. There are tall pillars and arches, and high above everything is the dome, so high that, as one looks up into it, its loftiest curves seem dim and misty and the eye loses itself in trying to see how high it is. Yet all the light of the great hall streams down from there, and down from there too comes the sound of the bells.

"The knights of the Grail are coming into the hall and sitting at two tables, long and curved, so that they make a great circle just under the dome. On the tables before them are cups, but nothing else. As the knights come they sing in chorus, and voices up in the dome and others still higher answer their song, while from the height far above them all still rings the soft voice of the chimes. And now the King of the Grail is borne in upon his couch and is brought to the highest place in the hall. Before him something is carried covered with purple cloth. It is the Holy Grail itself, and the time has come when it must be uncovered, that it may feed and strengthen its knights.

"But the King fears. It is when the Grail is uncovered and when it does so much good to all the others, that his wound always bleeds again and the pain of it is most terrible. Perhaps you think he is not very brave to delay what he knows he must do, but only think of that dreadful wound that can never be cured but by the one who is so long in coming; yes, think of the slow, weary years that he has waited for the simple Fool, and you will not wonder that it is a terrible thing to him to uncover the Grail again. But the voices up in the dome still sing the promise: 'Wait for the simple Fool, taught by pity, for him I have chosen.' The knights gently bid their King do his duty. He makes a sign to the boys who have brought the Grail. They uncover it and place it in his hand. Everything else in the hall grows dim, while one clear ray of light falls from the dome straight upon the Grail, and the red blood that is in it shines through the crystal of the goblet as if it were a light itself.

"A feeling of peace and gladness comes upon all, even upon the King. But now the Grail grows dimmer. The boys cover it again and the old light comes slowly back into the hall. All the cups on the tables are filled with wine, and beside each one is a piece of bread. It is thus that the Holy Grail feeds its knights. But the King does not eat, and suddenly he grows paler and presses his hand to his side. His wound is bleeding again and his squires quickly carry him away. The knights leave the hall too. The old knight is still watching the boy. If he is the Fool that was promised, if he is to be taught by pity, surely he must pity the poor King and he will ask something about him, why he suffers so, or what is his wound. But the old knight waits and the boy says nothing. 'Do you know what you have seen?' the knight asks. The boy only shakes his head. Then he has not been moved at all; he does not pity. 'Begone,' says the knight, 'you are good for nothing,' and he sends him away and is alone. And still from the dome, far up and out of sight, comes the chiming of the bells. If the old man could hear it right, surely it would say to him again: 'Wait for the simple Fool, taught by pity, for him I have chosen.'

"The Temple of the Grail is gone now. We are in the castle of the wicked magician. He has been thinking too of the young man - the boy - the Fool, who was at the Temple of the Grail, and he knows more about him than the poor old knight. He knows that if he is ever to steal the Holy Grail, as he so long has hoped to do, he must get this Fool into his power, of all people in the world. He has a magic mirror in which he can see him.

He sees that he has left the Temple of the Grail and is coming nearer his own castle.

"Now he needs the help of the woman, the woman who is sleeping and cannot resist him. He lights a magic fire, right there where you see that blue flame in our own fire, he speaks magic words, and the woman rises out of the very blue flame itself, and stands before him. But how different she is from that woman we saw among the Grail knights! She had no beauty then. Now it is radiant, burning, blinding. All that might make the beauty of a hundred women - the pride, the tenderness, the stateliness, the modesty, the fierceness, the gentleness, the rounded form, the glowing color, the waves of hair, the deep eyes, now flashing and fiery, and now soft and dewy - are hers. The magician smiles as he sees her. With her to help him, what can he not do? He tells her whom she is to entice into his power. She will not do it, she says. He reminds her that if she cannot entice the Fool she will herself be saved from all her wanderings and her weary life. He need not remind her of anything. She cannot resist him any more than she could resist the sleep that came upon her. What he commands she must do.

"Still the magician sees the boy approaching. He calls to the knights of the castle to defend it against him. They run out in a crowd to meet the Fool. He snatches weapons from the foremost of them and fights them all at once. Some he wounds and all he drives before him, for the knights that are in the magician's power quickly grow to be cowards. Not all of them together can keep him back.

"And now I see the garden of the castle. It is full of big, gay-colored, gorgeous flowers. They trail along the ground, they cluster upon the terraces, they climb upon the walls of the castle and of the garden, and they clutch at the ramparts and twine and twist about them. I suppose I must say that they are beautiful flowers, but they are not of the sort that I like. Anybody can see that there is magic about them. The earth and the water, the air and the sunshine, never would make such flowers. It might not be easy to say why, but just a single look at them is enough to make one feel sure that they are all poisonous. On the wall of the garden, with a sword in his hand, stands the Fool, looking down into it and wondering at the flowers. There were none in the least like these in the forest where he lived with his mother, and none about the Temple of the Grail.

"But what is this more wonderful sight still that he sees? Are the flowers alive, and are they running about and playing together? It is a crowd of girls, with queer, bright colored gowns that make them look for all the world like the huge flowers of the garden. They have just run out of the castle and they are all in confusion, and are crying and complaining because the knights, who were their play-fellows, have been beaten and wounded. Who is he that has done it? Where is he? If they could find him they would tear him all to little bits, you would think. And then they do find him. There he stands on the wall, looking down at them and wondering. And when he says that he will play with them instead of the knights, they forget all about everybody but him in a moment, and instead of quarrelling with him or trying to punish him for wounding their knights, they only quarrel with one another, because every one of them wants him all for herself.

"He has come down from the wall and they all gather around him, chattering and struggling for him. He does not seem to care half so much for them as they do for him, and when he sees that they will do nothing but quarrel about him he turns to go away again, but a voice calls him and tells him to stay. He turns again and stops, and all the living flowers run away, chattering and laughing at him. The voice that called him was the woman's, He is bewildered when he sees her. He has never seen such beauty before, any more than you or I ever have. For an instant he thinks that she is another of the strange flowers of this strange garden. Yet her beauty does not seem to move him very much. Perhaps that is because he is a Fool.

"But she speaks to him not at all as the other living flowers did. At first she makes him remember the old years when he was with his mother, how she cared for him in everything, and how she tried to keep him from knowing those things which she dreaded that he should learn. Then she tells him again how she died when he had left her. This, she thinks, with what she is to say next, may move him, and indeed it does, but not as she meant that it should. The great sorrow for his mother comes upon him again, and stronger than when he heard first that she was dead. He weeps now and throws himself upon the ground, and nothing can comfort him.

"The woman tries to console him now. She tells him that if he will but stay he may have all the pleasures of the magician's castle, and she will love him, she, the most beautiful woman in the whole world. But he does not heed her, the Fool - he is thinking of other things. He remembers the King and his wound. So much he remembers that he almost feels the wound in himself.

And as the woman bends above him there comes another thought. Nobody has ever told him, yet somehow now he knows, that it was she who tempted the King when he got that wound, just as she tries to tempt him now. I think that it is his own great sorrow that has made him know something of what another's sorrow must be, and when he has remembered the King and has felt the wound himself, all this has helped him to see and to know much more. Perhaps this is the way that he is 'taught by pity.'

"The woman cannot move him more, cannot tempt him, but now the magician himself stands on the wall of the castle with the spear in his hand. The blood still flows from the point and trickles down the shaft to his hand and stains it that deep, ugly red. He poises the spear a moment and then hurls it at the Fool. But it will not strike him. It stops above his head and hangs in the air. The Fool lifts his hand and grasps the spear. The blood from its point runs down the shaft and over his hand, and leaves it clean and white. He only shakes the spear in his hand, and the castle and the garden tremble and fall, as the fire here falls together, and they are gone.

"Once more we are near the Temple of the Grail. The place is at the edge of woods which reach away in one direction, while in the other are fields and meadows. It is spring, and the green of the trees is fresh and light, and the fields are covered with flowers. They are not like the flowers of that magic garden. Their bright little cups hold cool drops of dew, and the air is full of their perfume. The old knight is here. He has heard a sound like a groan from the little thicket of low bushes and brambles at the border of the wood. He searches, and brings out a woman - the same woman. She is still asleep, but in a moment she slowly awakes. She is no longer beautiful. She is out of the magician's power now, even if he is not buried under his ruined castle. She is ready to serve the Grail.

"The Grail! Alas! nobody serves the Grail now. The poor King, since that last time when the Fool saw him uncover the Grail, will touch it no more. He fears too much the pain of his wound. It cannot feed or help its knights now, and they cannot go any more to carry help into far-off lands. But to-day the King has promised that he will uncover it for one last time, for this is Good Friday, when the dove comes to renew the power of the Grail.

"While the old knight and the woman stand here, another comes toward them. He is a knight in black armor, with his helmet closed, and carrying a spear. 'Do you not know,' the old knight asks him, 'what holy day this is, and that none now should come here bearing arms?' The black knight only shakes his head. He sets his spear in the ground and kneels before it, taking off his helmet and gazing up at the point, from which the blood flows. The old knight looks at him and at the spear in wonder. Then he sees the blood, and by that he knows what spear it is. He looks again at the knight, with his helmet off, and now he knows him too. He is filled with a joy that he has not known these many years. Yes, the sorrows of the King and of the knights of the Grail are over now. This is indeed 'the simple Fool, taught by pity,' this is he whom the Grail has chosen.

"And now there comes the soft sound of the chimes to tell them that it is time for them to go to the temple to see the Grail uncovered. The old knight leads the way and the others follow. Through the woods and along the rocky pathways they walk, the sound of the bells grows plainer, and so they come to the temple. The hall is filled with the knights of the Grail. The King is borne in as he was before, and is brought to the highest place. The Holy Grail is carried before him with its purple cover. They all look at the King and wait for him. For a moment he wavers, then he springs from his couch - no, no, he will not uncover the Grail again; let him die rather; let them kill him, and then the Grail shall feed them and bless them, and shall torture him no more.

"They all draw back from him in dread at his look and his words - all but one. For the Fool goes straight to him and touches the wound with the spear. Instantly the wound is healed. 'You shall uncover the Grail no more,' he says, 'for I am chosen to be its King instead of you.' He makes a sign to the boys who have brought it, and they uncover it and place it in his hand. He holds it above his head and again the red blood in it glows and throbs. Down from the dome flies a white dove and rests above it. Before it, and before him who holds it, kneel the old King, no longer king now, the old knight, and the woman, for her too this new King has saved, for he has come, the best knight of the world and one whom she could not tempt. The simple Fool is the King of the Grail. The sound of the singing voices comes down from the dome, and from far above them come still the voices of the bells. Surely to any who could know how to hear it their chiming must say again: 'Taught by pity - him I have chosen,'"

THE ASHES

After the little girl had gone, I still sat for a long time looking into the fire. I was seeing pictures for myself, not now of the days so long gone by, but of days not yet come, pictures with the little girl in them. There, in the flames where we had seen so much together, I could see pretty clearly, as I thought, what she would be and all that she would be some time. But when I tried to see what she would do and how her lot should fall, the fire would tell me no more. Yet wherever and however it shall fall, may she not be a little better, a little wiser, a little happier perhaps, for knowing these old stories that have helped so many women and so many men before her to live their lives? Will it not be good for her to remember Brünnhilde's fearless truth, Senta's sacrifice, Elizabeth's constancy? And if to the thoughts of these she add Parsifal's lesson of compassion, surely then even a little of Eva's coquetry can do no harm.

And then I tried to see something of her knight. But the fire had all died down now, and was only a heap of ashes. I could question as much as I would, but there was no reply. Would he seek her out and come to her like Siegfried, through struggles and through fire? Would he find and help her in her greatest need, like Lohengrin? Would he only love her and sing a song for her, like Walter? Or would it be for her to help and to save him, like Vanderdecken? - Surely not like Tannhäuser. No, no answer. I stirred the ashes. Underneath there was still a bright, ruddy, friendly glow, but nothing more.

A clock somewhere in the house, with a low, musical note, struck midnight. But what was this other music that followed it? Was it again the bells of Monsalvat, this soft chime that came on the still air? No, no, only church bells far off, ringing in the New Year, Many times I had heard them and well I knew their sound. And all around those bells, I knew too, at this moment, there were noise and uproar and confusion, so much that those who stood nearest to them in the street could not tell whether they were ringing, just as many other sweet and pleasant things are made to seem lost among the coarse and the commonplace. But to me here, away from the vulgar crowd and forgetting it, the music came, faint indeed, yet clear and pure. I opened the window and the chime came plainer with the keen winter air, and the bells - I am sure of it - answered all my questions and rang a promise for the New Year and for all the years.

www.ingramcontent.com/pod-product-compliance
Lightning Source LLC
Chambersburg PA
CBHW020000050426
42450CB00005B/258